LAND TO WATER YOGA

Shin Somatics®
Moving Way

Sondra Fraleigh

iUniverse, Inc.
New York   Bloomington

Land to Water Yoga
Shin Somatics Moving Way

iUniverse books may be ordered through booksellers or by contacting:
iUniverse
1663 Liberty Drive
Bloomington, IN 47403
www.iuniverse.com
1-800-Authors (1-800-288-4677)
Because of the dynamic nature of the Internet, any Web addresses or links contained in this
book may have changed since publication and may no longer be valid. The views expressed
in this work are solely those of the author and do not necessarily reflect the views of the
publisher, and the publisher hereby disclaims any responsibility for them.

ISBN: 978-0-595-46637-5 (sc)
ISBN: 978-0-595-90932-2 (eb)

Printed in the United States of America
iUniverse rev. date: 2/25/2009

For My Students

Oh Fire awake … and be the guardian of our bodies.
—Sri Aurobindo
Hymns to the Mystic Fire

Contents

Introduction

It's not the head which has wings: it's the heart.[1]
—The Mother (Mirra Alfassa, 1878–1973)
The Sunlit Path

Yoga Means to Yoke and Be Ready for Surprise

Swami Muktananda, one of the first inspired teachers to bring yoga to the West, taught that we live with three illusions: that we are imperfect, that we are alone, and that we are doers. I offer this book in light of what I have learned about the intrinsic perfection of human movement from Muktananda; Sri Aurobindo; The Mother (who carries the yoga legacy of Aurobindo); Ohno Kazuo, my dance guru; and Moshe Feldenkrais, an innovator in somatic movement education. In trusting our bodies, we discover that we are all dancers; letting go controlling habits of mind, we experience our graceful bodies, flowing like water of their own accord.

Land to Water Yoga is a unique contemporary style of yoga, grounded in processes of *Shin Somatics®* as developed through our work at the *Eastwest Somatics Institute*. Much yoga today emphasizes physical competition, having lost the original intent of spiritual healing and self-awareness. *Yoga* means "to yoke": it signals our kinship with the environment and all forms of life. In practice, yoga can be a psychophysical means for transforming personality—progressing through enjoyable shapes and movements that anyone can do.

A *yoke*, in its positive meaning, is a bond or tie, a joining together or union. The Mother, quoted above, defines yoga as "union with the Self." For her, yoga is a generic name for processes whereby one transcends the limited ego toward a larger Self.[2] The translation of the Sanskrit term *yoga* is often stated in terms of union or unification. Linguistically, the kind of union elicited in the term *yoke* contains an element of surprise. I employ this element consciously in my creative use of yoga—bridging it with somatic movement education and intrinsic dance. I am interested in maintaining a connection to traditional yoga, but not in replicating the exact vocabulary. In the year 2000 I spent two months meditating and practicing yoga at Sri Aurobindo's first ashram in Baroda, India. It was there, in silence, in sight of the empty sandals of Aurobindo and the Mother, that I had my first inspirations about a yoga based on infants' movement development and somatic principles.

Yoga as informed by somatics—somatic yoga—evokes many possibilities. I link somatic principles to the traditional goals of yoga: clear seeing and a calm mind guide my practice. Being somatically awake to the moment, without stress or expectations, creates a condition for compassion toward oneself and others. *Soma* is the Greek word for the body as perceived by the inward eye, the experience of our own bodies, and it refers to the watery precognitive self. Soma is also the name of an intoxicating drink in ancient Greece. Pointing in this direction, Ohno Kazuo, the grandfather of Japanese *butoh*,[3] says dance should be intoxicating. Somatic modalities acknowledge pleasure and our need to be released from ingrained habits and limiting beliefs in order to heal. Gentle somatic movement modes encourage renewal through the relaxation response, self-remembering, and recovery of a more natural, original body. This happens beyond the will, but we can prepare for it.

Land to Water Yoga is conceived as a dance. When we peel away the social constructions of dance, we see a playful curiosity as its originating impulse. The same is true of yoga. Through the creative impulse of dance and yoga, the self moves past the limited ego. Adults can learn creatively through curiosity and can build skill with ease, discovering connections with the surrounding world and others, just as infants do.

Scratch the surface of traditional yoga asanas, and you will find somatic forms of human development underneath. Thus do we excavate the developmental soma of infancy in yoga forms.

Five Primary Stages

There are five primary developmental stages in Land to Water Yoga. Normal development of human movement contains at least five primary stages, which we can speak of in several ways. In this book I also refer to them as developmental movements, planes of action, movement processes, and sometimes I simply refer to them as positions. I introduce them below in the Five-Part Sequence.

The progression of Land to Water Yoga moves backward, or in retrogrades, from the most complex movement in terms of balance to the least: from walking to floating—from land to water. This progression gives us an opportunity to retrace our personal human development back to its watery soma source. We can also return to standing and walking along the same paths.

The five-part sequence provides a structural outline for the basic somatic yoga patterns, transitional patterns, and variations. These are all laid out in the table of contents and explained in the book. Your Eastwest Shin Somatics® yoga teacher can assist you in performing the patterns and help you discover habits that may inhibit your natural embodiment of the five stages. (Shin Somatics® certified teachers are listed in the appendix.)

Recovery of your natural body in these five primary movement stages may elicit surprising infant and childhood memories, excavating possible selves. Done with self-awareness, Land to Water Yoga can heal trauma. As you learn the five-part sequence, allow buried feelings to come to awareness if this seems right to you. Don't repress them, just let them be; and, as in a meditation, observe them, then let them go. When I meditate, I like to become an observer to my emotions, not getting entangled. You can let your thoughts flow by like a river. Cry or make sounds if you need to, then let this go also.

Use Land to Water Yoga to move forward in your life with trust. Cultivate compassion for yourself and others as you learn. Remember that yoga is a broad concept related to personal development and positive relationships. Shine your spirit in each moment of movement as you allow your body to morph—shaping energies and changing forms.

Five-Part Sequence

The five sections of this book follow the land-to-water sequence described below, moving retrograde through infant movement in the first year of life, from walking to back lying.

1. Standing and walking
2. Kneeling and crawling
3. Sitting and turning
4. Front lying with radiant belly breathing
5. Floating on the back and in water

Based in this sequence, Land to Water Yoga delineates somatic yoga patterns, at least three patterns in each of the five positions, with transitions, variations, and additions: It is recommended that the student first learn the five-part sequence as a flowing, connected developmental process—then use it as a structural basis for the yoga patterns. In Shin Somatics® Moving Way there are more patterns and process than I can include in this book. Eventually the student of yoga will be able to translate any asana (shape) into a somatic form, find the movement that flows naturally from it, and develop a creative sensibility along the way. The patterns illustrated here are selected to comprise a complete yoga with concern for *Shin*—the Zen word for center, heart, mind, body, spirit, and tree trunk—even as the trunk of the tree carries rings of life, leading to the center.

Figure 1. Christina Fraleigh in *Tree* with the hands expressing *I Am*.

Figure 1. *Land to Water Yoga* is circular in its form, moving from land to water and returning to land. It can also be performed the other way, beginning in the water, moving to land, and returning to water. The entire yoga described here can be performed in a comfortable studio or your own living room. *Water* and *Land* are images to guide the movements and meditations. In the full play of Land to Water, *Shin Somat-*

ics® teachers include water dances for partners who wish to support each other in warm water, such as a Watsu pool or warm swimming environment. These are part of Land to Water Yoga, but not within the scope of this book. Water dances develop the somatic experience of floating, craniosacral therapy in water, and the journey from water in birth.

Transitions and Variations

We have said that Land to Water Yoga is a process conceived in terms of infantile movement development. To underscore this, we pay attention to transitions between the five positions (or planes of movement) from land to water—and back to land. To bring awareness and creativity to the sequential process, I have created playful transitional patterns that lead from one stage to the next, so there are five transitional patterns to add to the basic somatic yoga patterns. Thus, you will learn many patterns that you can use in sequence or take apart and practice separately if you find particular shapes and restorative movements that are most helpful.

You will also find variations added to a few of the patterns. In this case, the benefits are explained, and you can choose to add the variations if they appeal to you. The variations extend the sequence considerably and also refine it. They can be added over time, as you learn the basic structure. It will take you several sessions to learn the basics and the variations before they flow together as a dance. Give yourself plenty of time to embody the whole. Release top-down controlling performance, let go of anxiety, and just explore the process in the "now." Surrender the goal of mastering the forms, and they will come to you.

Return to Land

Floating is not the final stage of Land to Water Yoga. There is no finality. Our yoga is circular in the return to land and awakening to dance. Returning to land, we move in wakefulness and consciousness of others: walking, running, and dancing—even as we carry the memory of crawling, sitting, and watery floating in the cells of our dance.

We carry the memory of water in all of our movement. Life begins in water, and only gradually do we move toward terra firma. One of the meanings of *nature* is "to be born," to emerge from water to air and breath. As babies, we can suck without being taught. The undifferentiated movement of flailing comes naturally, and nature is still at work in our movement as we reach for some shining object. Natural, fundamental movement patterns abound in the "P" words: pushing, pulling, punching, and pounding. Even as we learn a complex movement like grasping, the ability to do this is prefigured in human nature. These movements are panhuman potentials and naturally given—a gift of human life.

So also do we carry the memory of learning in infancy: how we learned to roll over from the back onto the belly, to extend the back, lift the head, and look out at the world from front lying. Using the strength we developed in the spine, neck, and head, eventually we learned how to sit up. From there we explored how to take weight into our hands and arms, how to curl our bodies to get the knees under us, and how to crawl. After that it was just a matter of time before our infant-self learned how to stand up using available affordances like couches or handy adults. We played with falling down and getting back up, sometimes in little jigs that were our first upright dances.

Walking comes last; it is a complicated process of shifting weight from one leg to another while maintaining contralateral upright balance. Of course, the infant doesn't think about any of this; it simply works it out through experiential learning, even as the ability to move is prefigured in the nature of the human body. We also recognize that there are different rates of learning and individual kinetic pathways. Nature seems to like variety.

Sometimes the ability to walk breaks down, through accident, for instance, or through trauma and psychic relinquishment. Concerning the latter, I worked with a woman in her fifties who had given up her legs, and only partly through accident. I don't know why her walk had disintegrated so dramatically, and I don't diagnose; rather, I work with what presents itself. She waddled from side to side in her walk, looking for the next place to sit down. She was also leaning forward and was in pain. I worked with her in my walking support group, meeting in the park for a short time three mornings a week. I taught her Land to Water Yoga in these short time spans over a period of two months, concentrating on balance in standing and walking, stretches in standing and sitting (on park benches), and adapting somatic yoga to her body and needs. I found myself helping her reclaim the power of her root chakra: the feet, legs, belly, and entire pelvis. We used breath, stretch, movement awareness, and the simple device of finding one's horizon in standing that I describe in this book. She learned quickly, surprising both of us with the improvement of her walk and relief from pain. Now she is experiencing more of the full somatic processes of Land to Water Yoga in a studio environment.

I like to teach the *land* phases of Land to Water Yoga outdoors when I can. Working outdoors is great fun, and we laugh a lot in support groups as people wake up to fresh air and greet the day and each other in the morning. We also practice awareness meditations, clearing the ego in silent sitting or walking to enter the day in peace and community.

Somadance

Eventually you will embody Land to Water in a way that fits you, with the basic patterns (or those you select), the transitions, and any variations you want to add. If you follow the lyric line of the five-part sequence that Land to Water Yoga defines, you will be able to perform a *Somadance* of about an hour's duration, depending on the time you spend in each pattern. Try performing the full somadance to music of your choice, but keep the performance free and easy. Pay attention to the feeling of the dance, not the look. This dance is not about being impressive or about stage presence; it is about celebrating full presence in movement.

Remember, you can also begin in water and move upward toward land. I like to do the full dance both ways, but I find that beginning on land gives me a chance to begin where I am, standing and walking, warming my joints, stretching my muscles, and experiencing the spaces between my bones in motion, moving gradually toward the peaceful state of floating, total relaxation, and self-remembering. Your somadance could vary considerably over time and in different settings.

You will make wonderful discoveries if you use the five-part sequence consistently. Let these five developmental stages (or planes of action) provide the basic structure for your dance.

Human Energy Field

Our human body exists in a field of energy and also generates its own related energies. Movement is made of body, shape, and energy. Thus, in Land to Water Yoga we pay conscious attention to energy centers—delineated as elegant color-filled systems of *chakras* in the East. We draw upon the body's basic energetic structure throughout our practice, extending its psychophysical implications in terms of health and healing, while using commonsense terms of somatic education. This book extends from yoga to dance in its interpretations of the human energy field as represented in chakras. At the end, we explore these in *butoh,* a form of dance that began in Japan and is now international, and we learn further how to unwind the chakras in seven stages.

Land to Water Yoga Patterns

Performing the Five-Part Sequence

Moving From Land to Water

Image
Imagine a song, one descending line flowing down through your land-legs to the crawling of your infancy and floating birth.

Benefits
1. Recovering primordial wholeness.

2. Learning to trust your body in descent to the ground and into water.

3. Note on healing: This five-part sequence outlines human movement potentials. Learn to perform this sequence with ease to experience your own potential and healing. Complicated patterns offer challenge and enjoyment, but this simple process has been more beneficial to students and clients at Eastwest than any of the more difficult patterning.

Instructions
1. **Standing and Walking:** *Walk into a clearing as you find your horizon.* Eyes look directly out with the chin neither lifted nor lowered when you are on your horizon. Roll your step from

heel to toe, not trying—just let it happen. We will practice the rolling motion of the foot in *Mountain Stride,* Pattern 1. I explain how to find the horizon in the *Mountain Stride* (see Figure 5) and at the end of the *Warrior Walk, Pattern 3.*

2. **Kneeling and Crawling:** *Descend to kneeling position* by reaching down with your hands and folding the body. In the folding, your toes, ankles, knees, and hip joints bend (or flex) softly. Fold your body with pleasure and get close to the floor, then take the weight onto your hands. If you keep your hips high and fold at the hip joint you will be in *Bear Walk* with feet and hands connected to the floor (see *Bear Walk* photograph and its relationship to *Downward Facing Dog* in Figure 13). Lower yourself to your knees, keeping the hands connected to the floor. You are now in position to crawl. Crawl by reaching one hand forward, and let the body follow through. Notice whether you are doing a counterbalanced crawl (contralateral) with opposite knees and hands following each other, or a homolateral crawl, moving same-side hand and knee together. Contralateral is more effective and natural. If you have difficulty with this, your teacher can help you fill in the missing links in your nervous system with somatic bodywork.

3. **Sitting and Turning:** *From crawling, lean to sit on the floor.* Keep the weight distributed on your hands and knees as you shift your hips to sit down to the side of your kneeling position. Go back and forth from kneeling to sitting to experience how your body translates weight from kneeling to sitting. Try both sides. Notice how your body turns, and experience how the ability of the spine to rotate helps you to move from kneeling to sitting.

4. **Front Lying with Belly Breathing:** *From sitting, turn and reach back to slide onto the belly.* Try it this way: In sitting, extend your legs forward and reach both arms back to the left side. Let your whole body spiral in the turn and reach to the left, then find the moment when you want to slide onto the front of your body. Your arms continue to reach forward

as you stretch out on your front, and your face goes down toward the floor. *In front lying, turn your head to one side and find comfort.* Let your arms come out of the reach to rest comfortably out to the sides of your head, with elbows bent. Breathe into your belly, as you root your navel to the earth and to your mother. (If it is uncomfortable to lie directly on the front of your body, turn onto your side. If you are uncomfortable connecting with your own mother, imagine an ideal mother.) Direct your awareness to radiant belly breathing. Relax into your breath as you visualize the color orange arising from brown and red. Let these colors morph, as they will, into the warmth of the root chakra, connecting you to earth, tribe, family, roots, and origins. Where does your soul rest? *Be here-and-now present*—alive in the ecstasy of time, not in the past or the future. Practice forgiveness toward yourself and others. The root chakra is supportive and relates to the feet, legs, and whole pelvis, including the belly.

5. **Side Lying to Back Lying and Floating:** *Coil up on your side, and roll onto your back.* Curl your body into a small ball, roll onto your side in fetal position, and then unfold your body as you continue to roll onto your back and relax into your breath. *Float.* Don't think too much about it. The feeling will come as you sink into the floor/earth and rest into your breath. (Bring the soles of your feet to the floor with your knees bent and facing the ceiling if your lower back is uncomfortable.) When you float, find a connection to your being beyond ego and individual identity.

6. Note: Further instructions for finding these positions, along with the yoga patterns that flow from them are included in the text. Photographs aid the descriptive instructions. In learning how to perform this five-part sequence you are embodying the outline or foundational structure for the entire yoga.

Rest and Float

Think about

Clarity and connectivity. Find your own way in the process of walking, descent to the ground, and floating on your back. How does your body want to move? What parts seem missing in your kinesthetic memory? How can you move more simply and ease your mind to recover the missing parts? Move with trust in your ability to find the most efficient and elegant solution for your body, your life.

Having performed and understood the Five-Part Sequence, you are ready to learn patterns and variations related to each of the five positions (stages). This book presents some fundamental patterns, but it is important to note that many patterns and variations can arise from these five developmental stages.

First Stage: Standing and Walking

Pattern 1. Mountain Stride Series

Image

Standing firm and tall, the mountain moves. Feel your connection to the earth through the root chakra, the energetic center of your pelvis, moving from the navel through the pelvic floor, extending down into the legs and feet—your roots. This flow of energy is warm in color, cycling up from the brown earth through the fire of the legs and pelvis. Breathe into the warm round bowl of the belly as you stride. The root, or first chakra, represents tribe, sexuality, family, and stability. When we lose power in this primary energy center, we fall down. Conversely, we can develop stability and confidence through walking.

Benefits

1. Finding full height in relation to one's natural horizon in *Mountain,* a traditional yoga pose.

2. Developing the self-reliant power of standing on one's own two feet in *Mountain.*

3. Stretching the backs of the legs, and associating balance with the natural curve of the low back in *Mountain Stride,* our way of taking *Mountain* into walking.

4. Rolling through the foot to practice the natural articulation of the foot in walking in *Mountain Stride.*

5. Practicing upright balance—of particular importance to dancers and for people as they age to prevent accidents from falling.

Instructions

Figure 2. *Mountain* (phase one)

1. Figure 2. *Phase One of the traditional yoga Mountain Pose:* Stand with feet together, heels and toes touching, and stretch arms overhead, as Jenny does in the back of this collage photograph, above. Cross the right thumb over the left as you stretch the middle finger upward, and bring your arms back over your ears. Jenny's arms could move back more with give in the shoulder, but she doesn't stress the position. This photo collage shows an example posture for four of the five developmental levels: standing, kneeling, sitting, and back lying. Front lying is not shown.

2. Figure 2. *Phase Two of the traditional Mountain Pose:* Open your arms apart with the palms facing upward, and gradually lower them to your sides. Feel the lower arm differentiate from the upper and come to rest near the widest part of the pelvis, the

greater trochanter. You will naturally come to your full height. Shift your balance from right to left very gently, then settle in the middle. Stand tall and still in *Mountain* as Maho does in the photograph below.

Figure 3. *Mountain*

Figure 3. In the photograph above, Maho balances on a log in phase two at the finish of *Mountain.* Her arms and hands could relax down by her sides, but she chooses instead to express them with power (Dancing on your Path Retreat, *Lucky Buck Ranch Retreat Center and Dance Deck,* mountaintop at Healdsburg, California, 2007).

3. *Mountain Stride*: Stride forward one small step as in figure 4 below, keeping the height and horizon of the *Mountain* as you lift the heel of the back foot, keeping the toes connected to the ground. Then shift to the back foot as you lift the toes of the front foot, and look down. Shift back to the forward foot and lift the back heel, as in the beginning. Keep the knees soft, and don't bend them. Remember, this is a tall mountain with soft knees and a flexible core.

4. *Summary of Land to Water Yoga Mountain Stride in ABA Form* (as in Figure 4 below):

   A. Stride forward. Keep the toes of the back foot easily connected to the ground, and allow the heel to lift up off the ground.
   B. Rock to the back foot. Lift the toes of the front foot. Bend slightly at the hip joint, and look down.
   A. Return weight to the forward foot, and lift the back heel as in the beginning.

Figure 4. (A, B, return to A) *Mountain Stride* in two versions

Figure 4. Two slightly different versions of *Mountain Stride* are shown above. Both of them illustrate this simple ABA movement pattern (First Version: *Land to Water Yoga* in a park in St. George, Utah in 2007. Second Version: *Somatic Yoga for Seniors* through the Institute for Continued Learning in St. George, Utah, 2008).

5. In the first version of *Mountain Stride* in Figure 4, Sondra and Dawn find an easy horizon looking directly ahead in A, and they bend only slightly in B to look down before returning to A. Sondra demonstrates her subtle mountain stride while Dawn captures the same lift of the toes, relaxed head, easy arms, and upper-back curve. In the small stride forward, they find their true horizon, floating the head upward and extending up through the heart space and mid-back. Ears and shoulders are aligned easily with the hips in A, as Sondra and Dawn find an easy upright balance on one leg before they shift to the back leg and lift the toes in front. *Mountain Stride* is beneficial for the practice of balance, thus for elders in prevention of falls. Sondra is sixty-eight and Dawn is seventy-eight.

6. In the second classroom version in Figure 4, Sondra encourages students to find a slight lift of the chest and extension of the back in A, before bending forward in B, hinging at the hip joint and keeping the back long. This will help them find a stretch through the hamstring and calf muscles in the back of the leg in B.

7. In still another version, students may explore letting the arms hang down in front by releasing the back into a rounded flexion rather then keeping it straight in B.

8. *Finding your Horizon:* Now, take another stride, and repeat the process with the other foot forward. Remember to find your horizon in the *Mountain Stride* before walking. This is shown below in Figure 5, as Sondra helps Howard find length through the back of his neck, ease in his throat, an easy jaw, and level chin (not lifted or lowered).

9. *Turning Variation 1*: Take the weight to the forward foot, and lift the heel of the back foot. Find a balance point, and then look around your shoulder, spiraling the torso slightly to look toward the lifted heel on the same side. (Turn toward the side of the back foot.)

10. *Turning Variation 2*: Turn to look at the lifted heel in back from around the other shoulder. (Turn toward the side of the front foot.) This is a further distance for the glance, requiring a

greater spiral of the torso and easy flexion of the spine. Balance improves with practice. If you have trouble at first, get someone to hold your hand as you turn.

Think About

1. Keeping your balance by spreading your feet easily into the ground in *Mountain.*

2. Standing in an easy vertical relationship to gravity, and finding stillness in *Mountain.*

3. Making friends with gravity, as you stand on one leg, then the other, without slouching into the hip joint in *Mountain Stride.* How does it feel to find your full height while balancing on one leg and then the other?

4. *Keep Mountain Stride playful,* and don't worry if you can't see the lifted heel of the back foot in the turning variations. This spiral simply indicates a direction. It is better to maintain an easy flowing spine than to stress in turning to see the heel.

5. In *Mountain Stride,* think about ABA form in music, eternal return in the philosophy of Nietzsche, and Zen circles where beginnings and ends meet.

6. Looking out on your *Horizon* as you keep the chin level (not lifted or lowered). Sondra helps Howard find his horizon for walking in Figure 5 below. In order to assist Howard, Sondra must be on her own horizon. Finding the *Horizon* is further explained in Pattern 2, *Warrior Walk.*

Figure 5. *Horizon*

Figure 5. *Somatic Yoga for Seniors* through the Institute for Continued Learning in St. George, Utah, 2008.

Use walking to rest between phases of this process. When you have been stand-ing for a while, walking is relaxing.

Figure 6. *Mountain Series* morphs into *Walking on your Horizon*

Figure 6. Appreciation for land, air, and water is the beginning point of Land to Water Yoga. In this photo collage, we see the entire *Mountain Series* as it leads into walking. The arms stretch high around the ears, then open wide to the side with palms up. Finally, they descend, and the shoulders settle down. This lifts the torso high over the legs, as the body aligns without effort, carrying this sense of upright ease into walking. Through the *Mountain Series,* the back comes into an easy neutral extension, the head balances easily on its axis, and the eyes look out directly toward the *Horizon.* The head is heavy when it hangs, but when it balances atop its axis, its weight is distributed throughout the body, along the flowing spine (St. George, Utah. *Shin Somatics®* Workshop, *Land to Water Yoga,* 2007).

Figure 7. Preparation for walking in the park

In Figure 7, students use tables and benches as props for rotating the spine and stretching the shoulders in the first photograph. In the second one, we see students reaching high to lift the rib cage and practice balance. In the last photograph, Kelly stretches the "walking muscle," the psoas, which connects the torso with the leg (lesser head of the femur in the groin) through the low back. She protects her low back by holding the upper leg in an easy diagonal position.

Moving Back:

At twelve months, the baby can combine action, words, and expression. He can explore boundaries, balance, energy, time, and space. The pull of gravity has become second nature, as he continues to develop an upright relationship with earth and heaven, land and air. He moves up, down, and around with ease. He is learning how to walk. It is never too late for adults to recover a friendly relationship to gravity in learning how to walk.

At eleven months, the baby negotiates a dance of balance. Standing is a miracle that involves all of the body's balancing abilities. Babies develop naturally and at different rates when given a supportive environment without controlling interference. Adults can assist best through playing with infants, noticing what the baby already does and is seeking to learn, having fun with them, and not instructing. Adults can also assist themselves in relearning movements that are a natural part of human development. Many eleven-month-olds can walk with one hand on a platform. It is best to let the infant discover walking without "showing" them how. The eleven-month-old can squat, stand, crawl, and creep in patterns. Human movement potentials unfold naturally in the infant.

At ten months, the baby increases leg mobility, moving into and out of sitting postures easily. He practices falling down in preparation for standing and walking. He babbles a lot, vocalizing with expressive hand movements, pinching and pointing. He can move backwards and likes to slide down stairs.[4]

Pattern 2. Dancer

Figure 8. *The Dancer*

13

Image

Figure 8. Dazzling, the dancer balances on one leg, eyes focusing outward in line with her outstretched arm and hand. On the free side, (s) he catches the front of her foot from behind and arches into arabesque, closing a circle of energy with the hand and foot. Jenny balances in the traditional yoga *Dancer* in the back, as the others are coming up progressively from water to land: Erin in the front begins to roll over from back lying, Sondra in the middle is coming up through the side to sitting, and Danielle, already in sitting, begins to crawl before standing. Shortly, she will stand in the *Dancer* asana. *Asana* means posture or pose in Sanskrit (Somatics Class, SUNY Brockport, 2006).

Benefits

1. Balancing with the back in extension while reaching outward into space.

2. Focusing the eyes for balance.

3. Developing courage in a challenging posture and practicing self-forgiveness in occasional loss of balance.

Instructions

1. Balance on one leg, eyes focusing outward in line with your outstretched arm and hand.

2. On the free side, catch the front of your other foot from behind, and arch into arabesque.

3. As you link the hand and foot, equalize the pull between them for balance, and look at single spot directly in front of your horizon for balance. Notice, in Figure 8, that Jenny stretches her forward arm on her horizon and takes her eyes there also. This brings her arm in back to the horizon and also the lower leg on the lifted side.

4. *Rest*, and when you return to the *Dancer*, find an interesting variation by taking your whole horizon down, pointing the outstretched hand and fingers down in front of you at about a forty-five-degree angle. The lifted knee will thus tilt up as the torso goes down. Use spotting with the eyes (looking at a single spot) for balance.

Think About

Accepting the experience of teetering and letting go of blame—gathering up the posture in ever-new approximations of the dance. Breathe easily, since there is a tendency for people to hold their breath in the dancer. Holding the breath does not aid balance; breathing softly and deeply does.

Rest this posture by walking freely.

Flamingo Variation

From standing on both feet, grasp one knee and squeeze it toward the chest. This takes the back and leg into *flexion*—opposing the back and leg *extension* of the *dancer* in the previous posture—providing relief and countermotion. Do this on both sides and at a pace that feels good to you. This leads to a walking movement (a slow pace) with a knee squeeze. Keep it free and exploratory. Many people find relief from back discomfort in the *Flamingo.*

Rest this process by walking freely.

Stork Dance Variation

Continue the walking motion developed in the *Flamingo,* but pace even more slowly. Come up on the balls of the feet, one foot at a time, and then descend to put the heel down, one foot at a time. Lift both elbows at once as you come up. Then press the shoulders, elbows, and wrists down toward the floor, as you descend into the heel and bend the knee. Remember, take one foot at a time, so you can walk. Keep it playful and don't worry about being correct. Find your own *Stork Dance* and experiment with flowing motions in the articulation of arms, elbows, and shoulders. Let them be asymmetrical at times, and tilt the body to the side once in a while.

Figure 9. *Stork Dance*—how walking becomes dancing

Figure 9. In this walking dance pattern, Sarah lifts the elbows, steps forward on the ball of her foot, then lowers her heel and lifts her back leg to the front as she also looks down. Sondra is shown in the next phase of the movement, lowering the elbows and pressing down with the wrists as she steps onto the front leg. Her bent back knee will then lift to the front. Sarah and Sondra make the movement smooth and allow freedom of interpretation in the dance (*Eastwest Workshop,* SUNY Brockport 2006).

Rest through walking or lying down with knees bent and the soles of the feet on the floor as you prepare for the Warrior Walk.

Pattern 3. Warrior Walk

Moving Somatically Through Yoga to Walking

Image

My body is made of sea and sky. My body is made of earth; my feet are soft and strong. I walk in the power of my feet. My arms extend out from my heart, the central organ and chakra of my body. I can paint the air in many colors with my arms. My heart is pink with giving and vivid green in the springtime of receiving. I float my head upward through the crown lotus toward the heavens.

Benefits

1. This sequence deeply engages the psoas muscle to provide more power and ease in walking. Feldenkrais Awareness Through Movement®, Shin Somatics® and traditional yoga warrior poses inspire it. You might want to look up Warrior 1 and 2 in *Yoga the Iyengar Way*[5] to see the relationships.

2. The psoas's connection through the spine and pelvis into the lesser trochanter of the leg can be brought to awareness in this Shin Somatics process *Warrior Walk*. The psoas and its attendant structures travel through the center of the body, from the middle of the spine, through the pelvis, to the femur, connecting the torso and the legs. As the psoas interacts with the primary breathing diaphragm, it also activates the heart center and thus the arms, which are an extension of the heart.

3. You can also use this lesson to get the feeling of the power and freedom of the neck and back in extension, and the origin of the psoas in the spine through the curve of the back. At the same time, the front of the body can sense its relationship to the whole movement, and does not sag forward. It is not that the abdomen is held. It is engaged naturally through the movement.

Figure 10. *Warrior* process to empower the legs, back, and arms

Figure 10. The above sequence of photographs is based on the traditional yoga *Warrior*, as preparation for the *Warrior Walk*. The *Warrior* is explained as a somatic movement pattern or process, and not a single posture, in the instructions below (*Somatic Yoga for Seniors* through the Institute for Continued Learning, St. George, Utah, 2008).

Instructions

1. Move gradually into the *Warrior* through a repetitive, gentle pattern: Move the legs wide apart, back foot turned in, and front foot pointed straight forward. Leave the torso facing front, and don't turn it yet toward either leg. Allow yourself to experience the position for the legs, incrementally. Take your time, and do this on both sides of the body, becoming familiar with the difference between right and left.

2. *Rest in standing* with the feet more or less parallel. Then go back to the wide apart warrior base, with the back foot turned in and the front foot turned out.

3. Bend the knee over the turned-out foot (with slow repetition) and, finally, keep it centered over the ankle. Extend the arms and hands, palms up, out to the sides at shoulder level (use gentle repetition without force.) Feel the arms root through the heart center. Keep the gaze and torso forward as in the first photograph, above.

4. Turn the torso, with outstretched arms, to the side, and face the bent knee. Then bring it back to the front. You will be rotating the entire torso: Face side, front, and side while the legs remain strongly rooted. Do this a few times in a gentle repetitive pattern.

5. Rest by taking a short walk.

6. Then, reconstitute the shape. Turn the torso to face side over the bent knee. Extend the arms to touch the palms of the hands overhead. Look up at your thumbs (as in the second and third photographs in Figure 10). Let the neck extend as you activate its root in the spine and extend your upper torso. Lift the head back between the extended arms as you reach up.

7. Now, release the posture by extending the arms out to the side again, allowing the shoulders to settle down on the rib cage as the arms descend (as in the last photograph in Figure 10). In this photograph, Ali is in front and has let her arms down lower in the process, so you see more of the final phase through her. Others are just starting the descent of the arms.

8. *Take a rest in standing. Then sit or lie down.* Close your eyes and visualize the process you have just been through. Emphasize the reach of the little finger as you look up at your thumbs in your imagination.

9. *Stand up and do the whole pattern again.* Now that you know it, allow the *Warrior* to find its own dynamic integration. When you reach up and take the head back, don't just let the head fall back. Lift it back through the arch of the entire spine.

10. *Warrior Walk:* Walk after performing the *Warrior.* Feel the power of your legs and upper body come naturally to the walk, since the psoas muscle, the feet and legs, the entire spine, shoulders, and arms have been enlivened in the *Warrior* and the *Mountain Series.*

Think About

The strength of the legs in walking, the length of the back up into the head, and the freedom of the arms as they swing from their root in the spine and heart chakra. Feel how easily the scapulae (shoulder blades) slide over the ribs in the swing. You don't have to do anything extra; rest into the strength of your feet and legs as they support you through the movement you have accomplished in moving somatically through the *Warrior Walk.*

Think about the abilities of the spine. Consider how the abilities of the spine to extend and rotate have been enlivened and brought naturally into the *Warrior Walk* through practicing the *Warrior* as a somatic process. Try the other abilities of the spine just for fun: forward bending (flexion), side bending (lateral flexion), and the sense of getting taller (growing), and shrinking. Go back into the *Warrior Walk* to see how it renews after exploring the abilities of the spine.

Finding Your Horizon

Balancing the head from the neck root and heart chakra: Stand in an easy position. Incline the head forward, bringing the chin in, and round the back forward through the upper vertebrae very gently. Return. Do this a few times. Now, incline the head forward enough that the chest recedes. Then let the chest come back to fullness as you lift your head. Extend your neck and lift the head back just a bit to look up; this will also lift the chest. Now come to a neutral position in the middle with your head balanced easily on your spine, and feel how your head can grow upward from its root in the heart chakra. This chakra also extends outward into the arms. So feel how they also relate to the balance of the whole. Sense your entire trunk, legs, and feet as a support for this balance. *Sense your feet in relation to your head.*

Further relating your feet and head, use this ten-minute process to fine-tune your horizon when you have time: Sit down with your legs and feet extended in front of you and comfortably apart. Rotate your head and feet together slowly in an easy circle to sense how they are related. Rest. Then circle the feet and head in opposite directions. Keep this easy, and don't stress if you don't get it right away. Now go back to the original circling, as you rotate the feet and head in the same direction, but make the movement very small and use just the front of the foot and the toes. Pay attention to the process, and see what part of the circle gets lost in your awareness. When I do this, the lower curve of my head circle feels lost. So I stop and practice this undercurve, the way I would a few notes on the piano when I need to articulate them separately. Be careful not to stress your neck. *Lie down and take a rest* to let this sensitive process integrate through the brain and nervous system, then move the circles around the other way. Be sure not to tire the neck, and take rests in between circles.

Stretching the back of the legs, practice this seven-minute process when you take time out from walking: Sit down with your legs extended in front of you a little wider than your hips, and reach both arms down one leg in an exploratory manner. Go just as far as is comfortable, a little past the knee for some people, and for others to the ankle. Don't be competitive with yourself; cooperate with your flexibility. Then reach both arms down the other leg. Do this with curiosity to find all parts of the leg in front and behind, gently brushing as you go. You will also be getting an easy stretch of the spine in relation to the legs as the back flexes forward with a slight turn, and your arms will be reaching, stroking, and patting—important patterns in infant development. *Rest before standing up.*

Balance your head on its horizon: In standing, have a partner observe you from the side, seeing the difference between a forward head (chin jutting out, neck strained ahead of the torso) and a neutral balance of the head on the return. The neutral balance grows directly upward from the root of the neck in the heart center. The ear is in tune with the center of the shoulder joint, not tilted back (from a lifted chin) or forward (from dropping the chin). Breathe into the heart center to sense how this helps to balance the head.

Let your body grow easily upward from your feet, and be on your horizon—*Looking Out*. Really see what is in front of you. Then turn your head to take in the environment all around you—*Looking Around*. Now find a neutral center, a divinely neutral center: Silent through your balance on your feet, your heart content, your jaw easy, your chin neither lifted nor lowered. Think of singing from the front of your throat. *This is your horizon.*

Figure 11. Connected *Warrior Walk*

Figure 11. Don't freeze your head on its horizon; keep it fluid. You can look out, up, down, and around, and return to the easy balance of the head on the neck. In this photograph, Michael observes Michele and Jackie as they practice being on their horizon with an easy, confident focus. He supports their walking as they join in energetic connections with each other and the environment (*Shin Somatics® Certification Workshop* in Brockport, NY, 2004).

Explore the Warrior Walk, and sense your head on its horizon.

Standing Meditation

Stand quietly contemplating the body's rootedness at the base of the spine and pubis down through the legs. Let the attention rise through the spine into the primary breathing diaphragm, and into the heart behind the sternum. Let your attention continue to move upward through the neck and head while you move the breath easily. Ask yourself where you feel the breath, just letting it move as it will. Let your mind clear through the gentle movement of your breath. If you want to move, let the movement come from stillness.

Stream color through the chakra energy system of the body: Among its many benefits, meditation teaches equanimity: this is balance, steadiness, and flow. Practice standing meditation to access the entire chakra system through the feet, in their relationship to the earth, up through the crown of the head. The feet, legs, and pelvis stream red to the orange color of the belly bowl, the molten liquid matter of emotion. The breathing diaphragm streams the golden richness of breath, moving the sun to every part of the body. The heart center is abundant and green, giving and receiving, and it can turn pink with love as it reaches to embrace through the arms and hands. We become more awake when giving and receiving find balance. The throat chakra streams from the heart into the neck, literally the nexus of creativity, speech, and poetry. The third eye in the middle of the head (the pineal gland in the middle of the brain) is a spiraling blue pearl of bliss and vision. The crown of the head streams aqua into the white lotus of wisdom, as the crown meets sky and spirit. This rainbow stream of color is a beautiful image to sustain embodied life. Trees also stream this wondrous energetic pathway and provide a sacred image for standing meditation.

Figure 12. *Standing Meditation*

Figure 12, *Standing Meditation:* Like trees, Sondra, on the left, and Celine, on the right, capture stillness and steadiness in standing, receiving color, streaming it in an energy flow from the feet through the arms and hands, neck, eyes, and head. (*Hawaii Retreat,* Kalani, 2006).

Walking Meditation

Lighter, easier, smoother, more grounded walking results from the related somatic movement lessons in *Mountain Series* and *Warrior Walk.* There is no one ideal way to walk, just the pleasure of finding your own upright ease in motion. Let your mind clear through the walking, with nothing to think about, and nothing to do. Breathe freely into the heart chakra, and send goodwill into the world. Experience *being* in your walk. Now you have the core support of the spine and the freedom that comes from having accessed the power of the psoas as it integrates the torso with the legs in *Warrior;* arms swing freely in contralateral relation to the legs. The head sits easily on the spine without stress—thus the eyes, as they look out, can easily guide the path of walking. It is significant that you don't have to try to walk any particular way. Your walking will find its own way and will change if you relax into it.

Transition: Bear Walk and Down Dog

Moving to All Fours

Figure 13. *Bear Walk* and *Downward Facing Dog*

In Figure 13, Danielle (in back) and Erin (in front) keep the hips high and folded in the joints, as they do the *Bear Walk*. Babies often do this *Bear Walk* when they come up from crawling in preparation for walking. Here Danielle and Erin are descending from walking to crawling, however. They move back through infant development from about nine months old to four months, allowing themselves to morph and remember. In the second photograph, Danielle, in back, is descending her heels into *Downward Facing Dog*.

Moving Back:

At nine months, the baby achieves new locomotion patterns. With *Bear Walk,* she can move through space toward her parents and her toys, or any shiny object she sees. Her communication skills are growing too, as she points toward what she wants, or gestures, as in a dance.

At eight months, many babies can come to *Bear Standing*, supporting the whole body on the hands and feet. They can also stand with support, banging on everything and pulling. They have developed responsive feet, and their flexible ankles and curious toes are precursors to walking.

At six and seven months, the baby can pull up to kneeling on all fours and practice contralateral movement, balancing one side of the body with the other. The baby strengthens core muscles for walking while practicing crawling on all fours. Adults can do the same.

At four and five months, babies prepare for a variety of crawling motions as they gain strength, pushing and pulling through their hands and arms, and using their legs.

In the second photograph of Figure 13, Erin transitions from the *Bear Walk* to *Downward Facing Dog,* as Danielle stops to ground the toes and heels in the traditional yoga asana of *Downward Facing Dog.* If she can get her heels down to the floor, that will be good, but if not, she will let them down as far as feels right, just to her edge and not into pain. From *Bear Walk* or *Downward Facing Dog,* they bend their knees and put them down on the floor—moving to all fours and *crawling* (Somatics Class, SUNY Brockport, 2006).

Figure 14. *Downward Facing Dog*

Figure 14. *Downward Facing Dog* is one of the most popular and beneficial of the traditional yoga asanas. Here, Sarah stands her feet just a little wider than the width of her pelvis and shoulders (her frame). We teach this stance for *Down Dog* in *Shin Somatics*®. It allows the heels to come down to the floor more easily and thus the whole figure to integrate with pleasure. Sarah achieves a wonderful length through her back and balance through the whole figure. Not everyone will have such an etched line in this position, and that's just fine. It is more important to start where you are. Learning as you go, build capacity along the way.

Perfect line is not the goal. Feeling whole and integrated in the movement is the goal (*Eastwest Somatics Brockport Tutorial*, 2007).

Second Stage: Kneeling and Crawling

Pattern 4. Spinal Waves

Image
Fluidity with Stability.
From kneeling, I can draw energy through my spine in undulating waves: *directly* from the tail through the crown of my head, *laterally* from side to side, and also *diagonally*—crossing the midline, from one hip to the opposite shoulder and ear, then moving through the other hip and shoulder in a crisscross pattern. Finally, I can connect these in a figure-eight pattern.

Benefits
1. Energizing the spine and central nervous system.
2. Bringing awareness to parts of the spine that may have forgotten how to move fluidly.
3. Gaining strength and stability in kneeling—using four points of support as a powerful foundation for moving the spine.
4. Exploring the abilities of the spine without the characteristic pull of gravity in the upright posture.
5. Strengthening the connection of the legs into the pelvis and spine.

6. Strengthening the relationship of the arms to the shoulders, ribs, and spine for improving walking and dancing.

7. Engaging the whole body in contralateral motions that have carryover in walking and improve connectivity in dance.

Instructions

Tail to Crown Wave:

1. *Inhalation:* Kneeling on hands and knees, begin with the back arched high away from gravity. *Inhale* and draw a wave of energy along the spine. Move sequentially from the tailbone through the crown of the head as you allow the back to "sway." The low back and belly relax toward gravity as the eyes look up.

2. *Exhalation:* As you *exhale*, tuck the tail under and arch the low back up away from gravity, allowing the motion to arch sequentially up the back in a wave. Extend the energy through the spine and out the crown of the head, as the neck and head flex forward and the eyes look underneath the body. You will be back to where you began in 1 and ready to inhale again while swaying the back sequentially from the tail to the crown.

3. Connect 1 and 2 above in an undulating repetitive wave pattern. Notice that in both 1 and 2 the neck and head are the last parts to move. The movement in both is initiated with the tailbone leading up into the pelvis and low back. Then it travels up into the mid-back, neck, and head. The difference is that in 1 (the inhalation) the movement culminates in hyperextension of the back (sway into gravity) and in 2, it culminates in flexion (arching away from gravity).

Sit back or to the side, and rest.

Figure 15. Tail to Crown Wave

In figure 15, Philip (right) and Kelly (left) are in the foreground of the class. Philip begins the *Tail to Crown Wave* by exhaling and arching his back away from gravity. In the second photograph, he draws energy through the tailbone, sending it toward the head as he inhales and lets his spine extend, giving his belly to gravity and filling it with breath. The body returns back through a wave that also begins with the tail, as the body empties all of its breath, lifting and hollowing. The body fills with breath as it sways into gravity and empties of breath as it pulls away from gravity. Thus, the wave returns to its beginning in a cycle that is repeated. Philip and Kelly keep this wave soft and flowing (*East-west Workshop* SUNY Brockport 2006).

Lateral Wave:
1. Still kneeling, and without letting the back and belly sag toward gravity, keep the back neutral and translate the hips to one side. Notice how the shoulders and head counterbalance this movement by going to the other side. Let this counterbalance of hips to shoulders and head create a wave where you forget which part is leading, because it has become a wave.
2. Go side to side, and let the wave lull your spine into relaxation. (You can do the same thing sitting on a chair.)

Sit and Rest. Close your eyes and allow time for the brain to integrate the movement you have just done.

Crisscross Wave:
1. Kneeling on hands and knees, be sure to balance the weight between all fours. Lean back a bit over the right knee, and draw energy on an inhalation in a wave beginning with the right hip. Tuck the hip under, then arch up across the back and out into the left shoulder, finally reaching the left ear

forward and extending the back into the ear at the end of the exhalation. Notice that you can take the weight forward into the left hand to increase the line of the wave. Inhale again, and return along the same path, tucking your head and ear under and shifting the weight back to the right knee as you extend the back into the hip.

2.   Do the same on the other side, and then see how you can connect the wave in a *crisscross*.

3.   Play to find a *crisscross* you enjoy. You can *cross* to the other side of the X at the bottom through the hips or at the top through the ears. The hips and ears guide the beginning and end points of the pattern. There are also various breath patterns that are fun to coordinate with the *crisscross*.

4.   Notice that the breath wave defined here completes an inhalation and exhalation in one line of motion or shift of weight (knee to hand, or hand to knee). There are other possibilities to play with. I like to cross over sides quickly and move through a diagonal shift of weight on inhale/exhale; then, on a second inhale/exhale, I cross laterally to the other side and shift weight through the other diagonal. I complete the entire X on two complete breaths. This moves the *crisscross* energetically into a figure eight.

5.   Can you complete the figure eight on a single breath, inhaling and exhaling?

6.   To summarize one contralateral weight shift from knee to hand, crossing from one side of the body to the other: The movement is sequential as in *tail to crown wave* above, but it is not symmetrical. Tuck one hip under and arch up the low back, allowing the wave to move up through the rest of the back and into the opposite ear as you extend the spine. Return along the same path by reversing the movement.

Think About

1.   Balancing the front and back of the spine in *tail to crown waves*.

2.   Relating the left and right sides of the body through *lateral waves*.

3.   Finding a smooth line of motion and shifting of weight while interlacing diagonal paths through the trunk in *crisscross waves*.

Crossing over the top and bottom of the X to make a figure eight.

4. Stabilizing your four-point foundation kneeling on hands and knees. Distribute the weight equally on all fours. Make sure your hands are under your shoulders and your knees are under your hip joints.

Pattern 5. Where Is My Head

Figure 16. *Where Is My Head*

Figure 16. Kelly, Jenny, and Lindsey play with crawling in relation to the abilities of the spine, neck, and head. They let the head guide the motion, as they pay attention to weight shifts between the hands and the knees, and see how grounding the toes (tucking them under) adds another dynamic to the crawl. In the last photograph above, Lindsey tucks under the toes of her left foot.

Image

I look around when I crawl. I turn to see where I'm going and what is behind me. I play with directions.

Benefits

1. Integration of the neck and head with the back and pelvis.

2. Playful activation of the spine in its capacities for side bending and rotations, as well as flexion and extension.

3. Facilitation of turning and looking behind. (In moving the head and neck from all fours, the back and pelvis can develop the natural responsiveness needed in turning around.)

Instructions

1. Look in various directions as you crawl; see to both sides; look ahead, and look behind you. Look over your shoulder and sometimes under. Let the weight changes happen as they want to, so you can look in various directions. Lindsey looks under her left shoulder in the second photograph, above. This shifts her pelvis to the side and rotates and flexes her spine with slight lateral side bending.

2. Allow the pelvis to make side shifts as the head shifts. The pelvis and head can move toward each other on the same side as the ribs fold, and they can follow each other in counterbalance, also with the help of the ribs and spine.

3. Don't require the neck to do all of the movement in an isolated way. Let your body cooperate and your back move, in order that you can turn your head and neck to the side, look up, down, and all around.

Remember to rest by sitting and getting off your knees when they hurt. You can do this exploration in phases, allowing yourself to rest before returning to the knees.

Think About

1. How your back responds to the various directions. See if it extends when you look up and around over your shoulder, and if it flexes when you look behind, under your shoulder.

2. What happens to your back if you look back and underneath between your legs? If you look directly up, then down and under you, this will arch your back up and down in opposite curves. In traditional yoga, this would be the cat/camel movement.

3. Find out how your weight changes from one leg to the other as you shift your focus, side to side. Think how weight changes happen easily, slowly.

Don't stress the knees by staying on them too long. It is too much to do all of the kneeling patterns in one day. Alternate them. The *Spinal Wave* patterns are more highly structured than *Where Is My Head*, which is freely interpreted as an exploration. And the *Tiger Crawl*, below, can be experienced as a way to test full-body integration after doing any kneeling pattern.

Pattern 6. Tiger Crawl

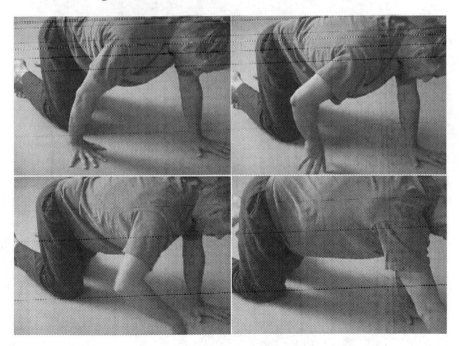

Figure 17. *Tiger Crawl*

35

Figure 17. Philip crawls freely with the image of the tiger (*Eastwest Workshop,* SUNY Brockport, 2006).

Image

My hands become soft paws. My body is supple. I flow; every movement is easy, and I have no joints. I can move easily down to sit on my side, and then return to crawling. I shift weight easily between my hands and knees.

Figure 18. Resting in Side Sitting

Figure 18. To protect his knees, Philip rests in side sitting before returning to crawl. He rests his weight into his hands and arms, turning into a spinal rotation. His movement anticipates the descent from crawling to sitting and the *Wrist Play* transition in between (*Eastwest Workshop,* SUNY Brockport, 2006).

Moving Back:

At nine months, the baby has learned hand, arm, and leg coordination.

At eight months, the baby achieves a variety of sitting positions and increased spinal rotation.

Benefits

Enjoyment of animal imagery in movement through kinship with cats. Incorporation of the eyes in seeing all around, remaining alert and alive in each moment.

Instructions

1. Let your hands become soft paws, and crawl on all fours, enjoying the movement of your back as you look around and remain alert to your environment. Find out how to sit and lie down on your side from all fours and return to crawl. This gives you rest from being on your knees and relates crawling to sitting and side lying, requiring you to use your whole body in smooth transitions, especially your spine and pelvis.

2. Dance the movement through your arms and into your body, lifting your paws slowly and using all of the joints in your arms: supple fingers, supple wrists, supple elbows, and supple shoulders. Then, let that suppleness ripple through the rest of the body.

3. Ask a child to crawl like a tiger, and let her teach you.

Think About

Keeping the movement smooth and connected. Try different tempos: fast tiger, lazy tiger, suspicious tiger, etc. Remember to rest on your side to relieve your knees and to renew the crawl when you return.

Transition: Crawl to Sit, Wrist Play

Figure 19. *Crawl to Sit*

Figure 19. Danielle, in front, goes from crawling to sitting on her side. Jenny, just behind her, is almost to the floor with her hips, and Sri, in the back, is already resting in a comfortable side sit with a flowing spiral line from her feet to her head, like Philip in Figure 18 (*Eastwest Workshop,* SUNY Brockport, 2006).

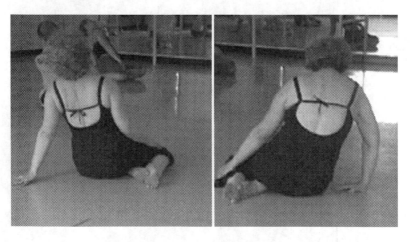

Figure 20. *Wrist Play* While Extending and Flexing the Spine

Figure 20. From kneeling on all fours, Sondra sits to one side, keeping her knees bent. She leans back into her hand and arm, as she extends her spine. Then she takes her weight into her right arm and points her fingers toward her body, stretching her wrist in this supination as she flexes her spine. She continues to play with taking her weight into the hand and wrist while extending and flexing her spine. She finds various places to plant the hands and eventually uses both hands.

As she ages, Sondra continues to keep her spine supple and her hands and wrists feeling good with this playful, easy pattern. *Wrist Play* is rehabilitative for repetitive stress injury of the hands and for carpal tunnel syndrome—because it involves the fingers, hands, wrists, and arms in relation to the movements of the back. See more about this below (*Eastwest Workshop,* SUNY Brockport, 2006).

To work with the suppleness of the arms in relation to all of the abilities of the spine, do this *Wrist Play* transitional pattern from kneeling to sitting.

1. Lean gently into the hands as you sit from all fours down to the side and your legs fold—both to one side. Use this opportunity to stretch through the wrist and prevent or ease carpal tunnel syndrome. With one hand at a time, point the fingers toward the back behind you, and gently lower the wrist to the floor. Control the weight so you don't take all the weight into the bent wrist. Take the stretch only as far as it feels good and integrated.

2. Begin planting your hands, one at a time, taking your weight alternately into each one. Plant your hands arbitrarily in playful placements. Point the fingers in various directions. Don't think too much—just do it.

3. As you continue, come up on your knees and transition your sitting across to the other side, alternating as you wish. Be sure to go to both sides of your sitting.

4. Begin to become aware of directions more specifically. Place your hands in front, behind, and to the side.

5. Now, plant both at once. Plant them sometimes close to you and sometimes far away from your sitting position.

6. Continue to transition from one sitting side to the other.

7. Become aware of how your back is working as you plant your hands and what kind of challenges you are giving to your wrist. Don't stress the wrist, but give it opportunities to settle and stretch in various placements.

8. Notice that when you look up toward the ceiling and plant the wrist, you are extending your back, and when you look down, the back has a tendency to flex. Let your whole back respond, and enjoy the tensile movement as your body arcs from the planted hand.

9. Plant the hand with palm down. Try contact with the fingers only, and then also plant the back of the hand. Keep careful attention on the wrist, so that you challenge it but do not stress it.

10. Think about the flow of movement from the hand and wrist into the back, pelvis, and legs.

Rehabilitation: This playful movement pattern is useful for rehabilitation of the hands and wrists from repetitive stress injuries, especially if the hand's contact with the floor is kept soft, supple, and alert to many directions and possibilities. And you can become increasingly aware of how the movement travels through the arm to the back.

Remember: Don't go into pain. Keep the exploration within a comfortable, pleasurable range. Try the fingers pointing in various directions, and take time to explore with both hands. Use the back of the hands as well. From sitting, you can lift on to your knees or ground your toes and push back on to your feet in a squat, as Meredith does in the last photograph below.

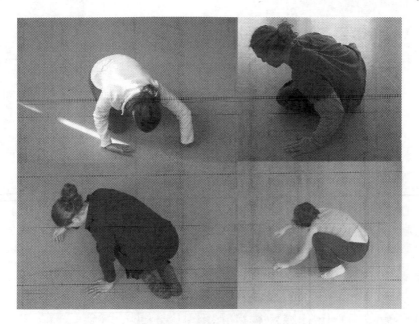

Figure 21. *Wrist Play*

Figure 21. (Clockwise) Sarah, Philip, Jenny, and Meredith in variations of *Wrist Play*. Students are exploring from sitting, kneeling, and squatting positions (*Eastwest Workshop*, SUNY Brockport 2007).

Moving Back:

At seven months, baby pushes and slaps the floor.

At six months, baby falls in and out of sitting.

Third Stage: Sitting

Pattern 7. Dolphin Dive, Dolphin Breach

Image

Dolphins at play give an image of ease and well-integrated flow. This pattern places a restriction on spinal flexion through the position of the arms, as they are held close to the torso. This position of the arms has a tendency to protect the low back. The dolphin pattern is thus not totally free, but has the advantage of being well integrated.

Benefits

Creates fluidity of motion in the spine with flexion and extension in balance. Counterbalance of arms being held down and back encourages even distribution of movement along the spine and adds strength to the movement. *Dolphin Dive* flexes the spine; *Dolphin Breach* returns the spine to extension. This creative yoga pattern aids shoulder rotation and length in the neck.

Instructions

1. Sit with both legs extended to the front, the back and neck long, eyes focused on your horizon directly in front of you. The chin is neither lifted nor lowered when you are on your horizon; thus, the head balances on the spine. Lace fingers

together behind your back, and press the palms down toward the floor with the arms extending down the sides.

2. *Dolphin Dive: Inhale* in preparation, then move on the *exhalation*, tucking your chin as you gently dive forward—leading with the head and curving the spine. Stay low on this same *exhalation*, and pause. Continue to stay low as you *inhale*, filling your flexed spine with breath; then pause again.

3. *Dolphin Breach: Exhale* and roll back up to the beginning. Extend the neck, as you return to center and press the palms of the hands down toward the floor. Don't hyperextend the neck; just return to neutral, looking on your *Horizon*.

4. Repeat.

5. *Dolphin Dive, Dolphin Breach* is performed in two complete breaths, including the preparation on an inhalation. Notice that you are required to breathe deeply while the torso is flexed in *Dolphin Dive*, pausing at the end of an exhalation. Then you inhale and pause again before coming up for air in *Dolphin Breach*.

Think About

1. Keeping your neck easy and free in the motion.

2. Doing less and maintaining a center as you move.

3. Pressing the palms down toward the floor to maintain a sweet tension between the spine, shoulders, and arms. Use this tension to help you return to center. Feel how the back is both stretched and protected through the position of the arms as you move.

4. How the movement connects in a cycle and creates a feeling of flow.

5. How this wave of the spine is different from the ones you learned in kneeling.

6. Inhaling through the nose and exhaling through the mouth at the beginning and, eventually, breathing easily and completely through the nose.

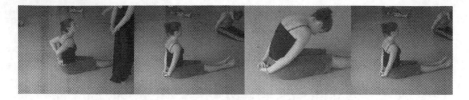

Figure 22. *Dolphin Dive, Dolphin Breach*

Figure 22. Danielle learns how to challenge her breath and protect her spine in *Dolphin Dive, Dolphin Breach.*

(1) In the first photograph, Sondra shows Danielle how to lace the fingers and turn the palms down. (2) Danielle begins on her *Horizon* in the second photograph, presses the palms toward the floor, and inhales. (3) In the third photograph, she dives forward, exhaling with the chin tucked in, and pausing low. She inhales while staying low with the back rounded forward in flexion. She pauses again, holds her breath a moment, and lets the back of her neck and head relax forward even more. (4) To finish, she exhales and presses the palms down to bring her back upright, returning to the beginning, as shown in photograph four.

Notice at the beginning and the end of the pattern (photographs 2 and 4) how Danielle's shoulders align beautifully over her hips when she is upright and reflecting her horizon. She keeps her legs and knees relaxed rather than trying to straighten them. You see Jenny in the corner of the second photograph, ahead of Danielle and already in the forward phase of the movement. The back of Jenny's neck relaxes forward, the tension in her arms creating a loop of energy that holds the low back in an integrated relationship to the whole of the spine. The arms gratefully splint the forward bending, so the breath can motivate and fill the core of the torso (*Eastwest Workshop,* SUNY Brockport, 2006).

Pattern 8. Bending Bamboo

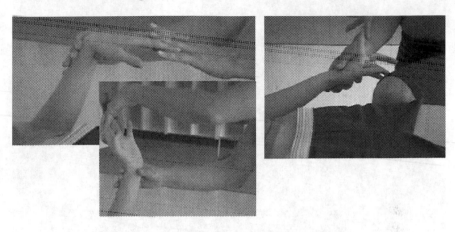

Figure 23. *Bamboo Fingers*

Figure 23. *Bamboo Fingers* in bodywork (*Shin Somatics*® Teaching Through Touch Practicum, SUNY Brockport, 2006).

Image
Bamboo in the wind, like the fingers or limbs of the body speaking in one direction: "You can bend me, but I will not break."

Benefits
1. Flow through the hands, fingers, and limbs.
2. Playful bending with the pleasure of reaching the hands and arms into space.

Figure 24. *Bending Bamboo* to the Side

In Figure 24, Danielle, in the foreground, extends her arms and legs and lets her body sway in *Bending Bamboo*. This is a perfect opportunity to practice side bending. Even though her arms are extended in opposite directions, both arms sway to the right in the lateral bend of her torso. She can continue to freely explore the sway of the arms and torso, paying attention to the feeling of the movement and letting the arms find their way intuitively. There is no "right" position for the arms—just the freedom of swaying while the sitting position provides a solid base of support (Somatics Class, SUNY Brockport, 2006).

Instructions

1. *Sway:* Choose a sitting position that feels solid and good to you, then reach your arms into space, and begin to sway the torso so that the arms arc and bend in the same direction. Let the arms sway with the movement of the torso. Don't think

about it. Just do this simple movement until it begins to move you. Then, use the bending joyfully. The legs can be out in front of you or open wide as you see above, or the soles of the feet could be together. The important thing is to have a base of support that is symmetrical and feels rooted. The arms could be close together, or stretched wide, as you see in the photograph above. Keep the arms soft as they sway, and find ease through the elbows and wrists.

2. *Bamboo Fingers:* Work with a partner to give the hands, wrists, and fingers some gentle motions, as in the somatic bodywork photographs above. Provide support for your own sitting or kneeling position as you work to find the bamboo nature of your partner's hands and fingers. Keep the exploration playful and pleasant. Take about five minutes with each hand, and then switch partners. *Bamboo Hands* is not so much about stretching as finding an easy range of motion and moving the hands and fingers away from their everyday habits.

3. *Rest:* Both partners should lie down and rest before continuing, so that the nervous system has a chance to replenish itself through the healing response of the relaxed bodywork.

Think About

Bamboo bending in the wind: strong and yielding at the same time. Think about the arms and hands reaching out from the central organ of the body, the heart. As an option, think of ending the *Bending Bamboo* exploration with the arms held close to the body, wrapping and self-embracing, still expressing the heart space.

Pattern 9. Bound Angle to Leg-Over Inward Twist

Figure 25. *Bound Angle Preparation* and *Twisting Patterns*

In Figure 25, Sarah opens her legs wide with feet in standing. She turns to face the right and looks up into her right hand with the arm extended high. At the same time, she increases the twist by reaching her left hand under her left leg with the fingers pointing in toward her sitting bone. This rotates the left arm inward and rotates the spine to the right as well.

Note on hand placement: The hand on the floor turns inward in supination. If you have trouble finding the hand position: Lift the hand up in front of you with the palm down, then turn the fingers toward your navel. Keep the hand in this position as you place it on the floor and tuck it close to your leg. It doesn't matter if it won't go under your leg. Put it where you feel a little challenge, but not too much. Maybe just the tips of your fingers will touch the floor in this position. This is fine. Rotating the shoulder inward helps you move the hand under the leg.

Bound Angle yoga posture (not shown) is simply sitting with the bottoms of the feet together. (In *Eastwest* workshops, we also call it *Frog.*) The arms can rest anywhere, as long as the back is easily upright. Don't make the common mistake of grabbing the ankles or feet and pulling on them. This distorts the easy open fall of the knees when the feet are placed together in *Bound Angle.*

Bound Angle Preparation that Sarah shows above (figure 25) is much more difficult than the *Bound Angle* posture itself. The preparation opens the hip joints for *Bound Angle,* making it easier to sit comfortably with the feet together, and allowing the knees to open wide apart. *Bound Angle Preparation* also makes any twisting pattern easier to perform. In Shin Somatics® processes, we pair *Bound Angle Preparation,* and *Bound Angle* with *Twisting Patterns* because they flow together logically through a concern for what is happening in the hip joint in all of these patterns. The patterns all aid each other.

Figure 26. *Lifted Bound Angle*, with feet held off the floor, heels and wrists together

In Figure 26, above, you see how *Bound Angle* can be lifted off the ground at the end, to create equanimity in sitting while engaging abdominal strength. (*Bound Angle Preparation* and *Lifted Bound Angle*, Eastwest Workshop, SUNY Brockport, 2007).

Figure 27. *Leg Over Inward Twist*

Figure 27. These seniors show elegant form: Maxine, in the first photograph; Valeria (in front) with Chris (behind) in the second photograph; and Jim, in the last photograph, perform the *Leg Over Inward Twist.* They continue to learn and practice yoga well into their seventies and eighties (*Somatic Yoga for Seniors,* Institute for Continued Learning, St. George, Utah 2008).

Image

Divine neutrality in turning and twisting to look behind. I sit tall, grow and turn into the space behind me—using my knee and elbow as an anchor. I turn and look back without regret. My inner core is soft and calm.

Benefits

1. Stretching the outward rotating muscles of the hip that are often implicated in back and hip pain.

2. Improving digestion through an easy twist of all of the internal organs.

3. Facility in turning the head and neck.

4. Learning how to soften and rotate the rib cage.

5. Looking into the past while letting go.

Instructions

1. *Prepare* by stretching both legs out long in front of you and sitting up tall.

2. *Phase 1.* Cross the right leg over the top of the left by bending the knee and turning it outward (not shown in Figure 27). The right ankle crosses over the midline of the body just above the left knee, and the right foot is not yet planted on the floor. Press down on the outward-turned right knee just slightly, until you feel a stretch across the back of the buttocks on that side. Stay there for a while in this first simple phase, and enjoy the stretch of the outward rotators.

3. *Phase 2.* Now place the right foot on the floor, crossing over the knee of the extended left leg, and plant the foot firmly. If

you can't get the entire sole of your foot on the floor, just get a feeling for grounding as much of the foot as possible.

4. *Turn around* to look over your right shoulder as you embrace your right knee with your left arm, as in Figure 27.

5. *Maintain equanimity* as you breathe into the twist, and hold for about five breath cycles.

6. *Rest the position.*

7. *Try the other side.*

8. *Return to the first side,* and see if it is easier to maintain the twist now that you have experienced it once.

9. *Return to the second side,* and feel yourself develop a neutral ease in the twist.

10. *Bathing Beauty Variation:* You can lean into the back hand as you take it further behind you a little, and lift your chin slightly as you turn the head. Keep the back long, however, and don't use the lean to collapse the shape. Use the lean to indulge yourself, and don't forget to smile.

Think About

1. Developing neutral ease in the twist.

2. Using your eyes to look back and see around behind you.

3. Bringing the opposite knee and elbow together as you hug your leg.

4. Breathing into the twist.

5. Keeping the back tall.

6. Finding the expressive difference between an upright back and leaning into the *Bathing Beauty.*

Cow Face Variation

Figure 28. *Cow Face*

In Figure 28, Sondra adds another sitting posture. *Cow Face* is a traditional yoga asana that stretches the back into forward flexion while also stretching the outward rotators of the hips. The knees meet at midline, and the lower legs cross over. If you are unable to touch the head to the knees, it doesn't matter; just let the back round easily forward as far as it wants to go comfortably. And if your hip flexors won't allow the knees to cross over to the middle, simply approximate the pose.

The main thing is to be comfortable and not to stress the lines of the movement. Find out how this posture fits your own body. Sondra is sixty-eight as she does this posture and plans to keep ease in her body throughout her lifetime with the fluid movement of Land to Water Yoga. She had back surgery for an old injury nine months before this photograph was taken. She uses somatically inspired yoga for rehabilitation and energy. She has also experienced how the pull of muscle on bone in yoga helps keep bones strong (*Land to Water Yoga Workshop*, SUNY Brockport, 2007).

Transition: Spiral Down to Front Lying

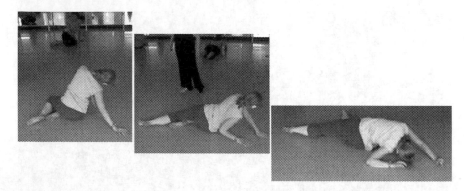

Figure 29. Spiral Transition to Front Lying

Figure 29. Kelly descends from sitting to front lying by reaching back and rolling onto the front of her body. This creates a wonderful spiral descent through the whole body. She extends her back leg and keeps her head and eyes focused down. (Completion of the movement, to rest in front lying, is shown in the next photograph.) Students make different choices in doing the downward spiral. There are options in the details of performing this movement.

The movement is also reversible. You can accomplish an ascending spiral by lifting the left leg up from front lying, crossing it over the midline, and following it up to sitting. To see this retrograde ascent, look at the photographs from bottom to top. *On the ascent:* use momentum and engage the deep power of your core to come up. *On the descent:* turn, rotate, and reach out through your core, as you give your weight easily to gravity (*Eastwest Workshop,* SUNY Brockport, 2006).

Fourth Stage: Front Lying

Finding Center: Navel Root in Front Lying

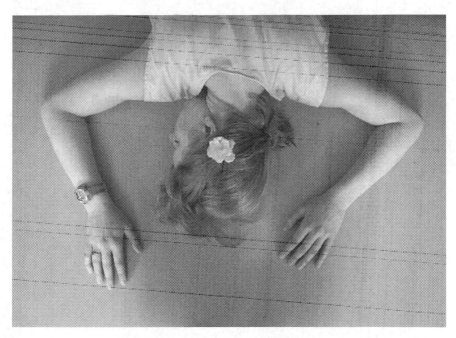

Figure 30. *Navel Rooting Reflex* in Front Lying

In figure 30, Kelly floats in front lying and sends breath to her navel. Feeling safe, she allows the earth to support her and evokes the innocence of infancy (*Eastwest Workshop*, SUNY Brockport, 2006).

Pattern 10. Barking Sea Lion and True Seal

Image

Imagine the belly as a source of power. Rooting the navel to land and water is good preparation for *Sea Lion*. Sea Lions are eared seals (or walking seals) from the family *Otariidae*. They are barrel-shaped marine mammals, adapted to a semiaquatic lifestyle. They feed and travel in the water but breed and largely rest on land, rocks, or ice. They are slightly less adapted to the aquatic lifestyle than are the true seals.

True Seals are more streamlined than sea lions, and can therefore swim more effectively over long distances. However, because they cannot turn their hind flippers downward, they are very clumsy on land, having to wriggle with their front flippers and abdominal muscles; this comical method of locomotion is called "galumphing." True seals do not communicate by "barking" like sea lions. They communicate by slapping the water and grunting.

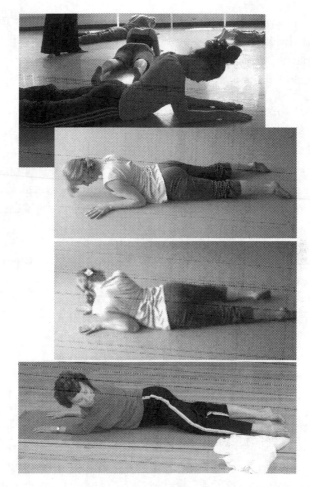

Figure 31. *Sea Lion and True Seal* (preparation and first phases)

Figure 31. In the first photograph, above, Jenny lifts her torso and lifts and drops her head in preparation for *Sea Lion*. Her forearms can fan out to the side, to the back, or forward (as shown here). She can lift and lower her head, take it side-to-side, look back, up, down, or forward. She can also drop her torso closer to the floor, as Kelly does below her, and remove most of the weight from her arms by not resting on them or pushing through them. (The arms can be anywhere; just don't support much weight on them.)

Kelly's *Sea Lion* drops close to the ground in the second and third photographs. Her flippers come in close to the body as her arms touch her sides, and the hands fan forward out to the side. As a sea lion, Kelly lifts her torso and places very little weight on her arms. She looks behind, toward her knee, as she prepares to drag herself slightly forward with her front "flippers" (hands and lower arms), pushing with her right big toe and the inside of the knee through her downturned back flipper.

Kelly can *pull* forward with her front flippers, and *push* forward with her back ones. She can move symmetrically or asymmetrically. She can balance one side with the other in contralateral diagonals, and she can go backward or roll to the side. She must *push* through her hands and arms to go backward. She can also contract her belly in a wave, as she grabs the earth with the front of her body, working in concert with the back, and using very little aid with her flippers.

She will think of using the core strength of her trunk, relating the back of the body to the front and the head to the feet. She creates a round, full, flexible feeling and keeps the movement playful. If she uses only her front flippers to move without using her feet, she will use her arm and belly/back strength to "galumph" like a *Seal*. No fair using the legs and feet on this one! Let them trail and flow, or flip in the air behind you, however they will (*Eastwest Workshop,* SUNY Brockport, 2006).

In the last photograph, Maxine, a senior in her late seventies, still maintains a playful relationship to yoga and movement as she explores the *Sea Lion* and *Seal,* looking back behind herself with a full rotational feeling in her torso and belly, as she rolls slightly to the right, dragging up her left hip and knee (*Somatic Yoga for Seniors,* Institute for Continued Learning, St. George, Utah, 2008).

Benefits

Core lift of the back and torso: Lifting the torso from the floor with little help from the arms requires core support of the deep muscles supporting the spine and torso and a feeling for the relationship of the belly to the low back. With the *Sea Lion* low-to-the-floor back extension, the large superficial muscles of the back also provide support. They contract when the arms lift off the floor to the front or the back.

Instructions

1. *Preparation:* Lift your torso and place weight on the arms with the elbows under the shoulders, as Jenny does in the first photograph, above. You can lift your head as in the traditional yoga shape called *The Sphinx*. Then drop your head down from there, and lower yourself onto your forearms, keeping them close to the body, as Kelly does. Now you are on your way from *Sphinx* to *Sea Lion*.

2. *Preparation:* Use the core strength of your trunk, relating the back of the body to the front and the head to the feet, as you lift the trunk slightly off the floor and remove weight from the arms.

3. *Preparation:* Try lacing the fingers of your two hands together behind your back in this front lying position. The front of the body will elongate in response to this "core" lift of the back and torso.

4. Use your front and back flippers intuitively to scoot forward and back, to the side, or around. See where you are going, use your eyes and your nose. Notice that you can *pull and push* with all of your flippers, moving with symmetry or asymmetry, forward and back, side to side.

5. Notice how your belly participates in concert with your back in your movements. Bring the belly/back consciously into play.

6. Now for the *True Seal*: Without grounding the feet, use your hand/arm and belly/back strength to "galumph."

7. To find variations, supinate and pronate the wrist, allowing the fingers to fan in various directions. This is not easy at first and requires accommodation through the entire arm and the elbow into the shoulder. So keep the various fanning directions small and playful without stressing.

8. Rest and try again. You will find it gets easier if you stop trying to make something happen and just have fun.

9. *Replant* the arms and hands in various locations to see how many interesting shapes they can take. See what happens when

you "belly wiggle" forward and backward, or do a bit of side-to-side "lolling about."

10. As you develop a feeling for turning your hands and arms into flippers, let these carry you in tandem with your belly/back. Remember to keep the movement round and rolling. No two people look alike in the *Sea Lion and Seal.*

11. *Rest* between your various attempts, and do less than you can in order to find spontaneity.

Think About

Keeping all of your movement playful and barrel-shaped. Not working hard at this, and making discoveries about what feels good—what feels easy—and what feels pleasurable. Doing the *Sea Lion and Seal* with children. They love to galumph and bark.

Pattern 11. Lazy Lizard Spiral

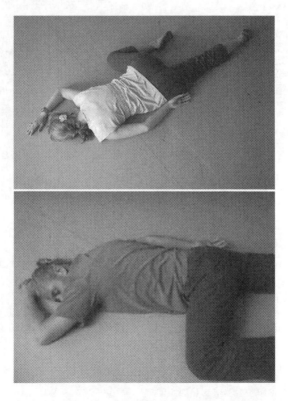

Figure 32. Kelly and Philip rest in *Lazy Lizard Spiral*

Figure 32. Kelly and Philip relax into the *Lazy Lizard Spiral*. The spiral pattern is created as the body naturally rolls a little toward the extended leg. The other knee is bent and lifted up to the side, with the hip lifted off the floor. The knee and elbow angles help to ground the movement. The rotation through the spine is gentle and well distributed along the length of the back. You can see traces of the rotations in the diagonal wrinkles of the pants and shirts. Notice that the arm frames the head in the direction of the turn. When the head turns away from the arm, the flow is less organic, even as this is a possible movement for some people. If you try the inorganic way, turn the head back for relief. Kelly and Philip contact their breath while they rest, and allow the belly to relax toward the floor and gravity (*Eastwest Workshop*, SUNY Brockport, 2006).

Image
Breathing into the belly while resting in *Lazy Lizard* allows the back a restful, rehabilitative pattern.

Benefits
1. Rotation of the spine in a restful position.
2. Back rehabilitation and pain relief, depending on individual conditions.
3. Teaching the hips how to rotate, or rather the entire pelvis how to rotate.
4. If the pelvis is stiff, unlocking it for better motion in walking.

Instructions
1. From front lying with your legs extended long, frame your face with your arm (look into the bend of your elbow), and put the other arm down by your side.
2. Bring up the knee on the same side as your eyes are looking; remember to look into the arm that is up around your head (framing your head). See Kelly and Philip in Figure 32.
3. As you bring the knee up to the side, the hip on the same side lifts up off the floor. This rotates the spine and the pelvis.
4. Note on knee placement for grounding the shape: If you bend the knee up and take it wide away from center, you will lose the rotation through the spine and pelvis. Keep the knee close

enough to the midline of the body that you achieve an easy rotation.

5. If you experience any pain in bringing the knee up to the side, or in the lift of the hip off the floor, you can put a rolled towel under the lifted hip to support it. Put the towel in the space created by the lift of the hip, and let the hip relax into the towel.

Think About

Breathing into your belly and relaxing the entire position. Stay in *Lazy Lizard* for as long as you want to. This restful position is rehabilitative for the back.

Pattern 12. Crab Connection

Image

All arms and legs—or rather, the arms become as strong as legs. The hands push into the floor, and the arms flex and rotate all of their joints. The legs find their knees and feel their connection to the hips.

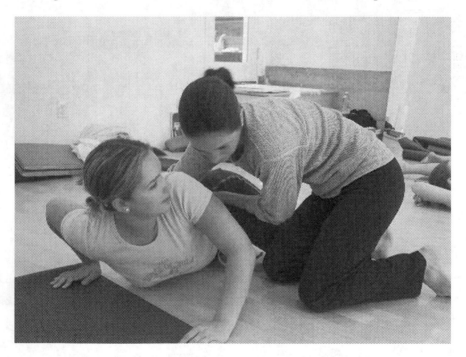

Figure 33. *Crab Connection*

In Figure 33, April assists Stacy in an infant precrawl developmental pattern, emphasizing rotation in the torso and flexion in all the joints of the limbs. Stacy looks back over her shoulder. We call this the *Crab Connection* because of the connection of the arms (through the hands) and legs (through the feet and knees) to the floor. Notice the flexible bending of the wrists, elbows, and shoulders and how the entire arm in its integration with the rest of the torso is used for support. The legs participate also, as the knees bend up to the side (as in *Lazy Lizard*). Here, Stacy practices rotating from side to side as she brings up her knees and lifts her chest, supporting herself on her hands. If she were an infant, in the next developmental phase Stacy would learn locomotion close to the ground, and then come up onto all fours to crawl (*Eastwest Workshop*, San Francisco, *Studio aov*, 2002).

Moving Back:

At six months, the baby continues to prepare for crawling through play from the prone position. She can fly like an airplane with full extension of the spine and has mastered rolling from the back to the belly. Flexible ankles and feet prepare her to move from crawling and creeping toward walking. She loves to push and slap the floor. She can play with sitting, falling into and out of it. This frees her hands for fine motor skills. She often likes to push with her hands as she scoots back on her belly. She can move from her side to her hands and knees and pull up to kneeling, bringing her legs under her.

At five months, the baby can roll over in a sequential pattern and, with difficulty, lift the head from side lying. She can rock on her belly and push up with the arms, also pushing through the feet. She likes to reach the hand on the same side as the body. She learns how to push up from *Sphinx* to *Cobra*—that is, from supporting the weight on the forearms to full extension of the arms pushing through the hands. Thus she has the basic rotational and pushing skills for *Crab Connection*. While she may not follow the pattern exactly, you can see elements of it as she plays.

At four months, the infant has learned how to take the spine into extension, how to flex from side lying, and can maintain the head in midline through support of the forearms. She can manage "belly

---

swimming" and can push up onto her forearms in self-motivated play. She can also shift her weight sideways from front lying. This prone position is fundamental to infant play.

Benefits

This movement pattern develops coordination throughout the body in a contralateral pathway, as diagonal relationships between the hips and shoulders develop in the movement. If Stacy (in Figure 33) were to sit up and relate opposing knees and shoulders, she would approximate this developmental pattern in sitting. If she were to replicate it in standing, it could carry her into the natural contralateral pattern of elegant walking, where all of the joints cooperate and move in concert—balancing the whole body as one leg replaces the other in contrapuntal forward momentum.

Instructions

1. From front lying, connect the hands to the floor out to your sides by bending the elbows. Then connect the toes to the floor by bending them. Keep the legs long to begin with, and just experience the power of your toes and feet through this connection and the power of your arms through the connection of the hands into the floor. There's no need to push hard; just keep a balance throughout the whole push.

2. *Mirror Limbs:* Next, lift the torso up, through the power of the arms. Rotate the torso from side to side, practicing the power of your arms and legs as mirror limbs—and like the crab, move in slow motion to experience all of the joints of your limbs, as you shift the weight from side to side, looking over (and sometimes under) your shoulder. The legs can remain long, or the knees can bend up to the side to create more rotation throughout the whole body. The toes can be flexed and connected to the floor, or you can release them. Try both ways.

3. We think crabs don't look over their shoulders, but what do we know? Just have fun as you play with precrawl movement through the image of the *Crab* in its profound and delicate connectivity and all of its jointed motion.

4. Stacy does not locomote forward or backward in her *Crab Connection*, but you can crawl (or creep) close to the floor from this connectivity. Don't try to figure it out; let your body figure it out spontaneously, like a baby.

Think About

Going nowhere and doing nothing, as you meander from side to side in one place, rotating the torso and connecting the limbs to the floor, integrating them through your core. Think about this equation for integration: *Integration = Coordination + Balance.*

Rest in (S)he Crab Spiral

To get into the *(S)he Crab Spiral* (not shown), look at Figure 32, The *Lazy Lizard*. From the *Lazy Lizard* position, fold the extended leg up underneath the bend of the top leg. Match the legs; they will both be folded. You will be looking into the frame of the arm that is up, and the other arm rests down by your side. This curled-up position is actually half front lying and half side lying. To get into side lying from *(S)he Crab,* see the description of side lying that follows.

Transition: Side Lying in Embryo

Push up from *(S)he Crab Spiral* with the arm in front of your face, and scoot the back arm underneath you to the front. This changes your resting position to *Embryo.* This is a simple change; just one motion will do it—if you find the connection between the push that lifts the torso and the back arm as it scoots under. There are, of course, many ways to lie down on your side. This way flows naturally from the curled-up, rounded feeling of *Crab Spiral.*

Figure 34. *Embryo* Transition

Kim, Fumiko, and Nancy rest in *Embryo*. You see variation in the way people come to side lying. Kim rests her head on the ground, while Fumiko and Nancy rest into their hands. In the somatics perspective, there is no right or wrong way to rest in *Embryo*. The important thing is to find floating comfort. (*Hawaii Retreat,* Kalani, 2006).

Moving Back:

In the first three months, babies express curiosity, interest, and plea-sure. Healthy babies let you know what they want. They can suck, roll their heads from side to side, explore all parts of their bodies, take a hand and foot to the mouth, and respond to sound. They can extend and flex their arms and legs. And they like to kick. By three months they can direct arm motion by reaching into space, adopt symmetrical postures, and flex in side lying as we see above, in *Embryo*. Babies can also maintain their heads in midline by sup-porting themselves on their forearms. This allows them to eventually sleep with their butts up in the air while resting on their arms and chest.

Fifth Stage: Side Lying and Back Floating

Pattern 13. Little Boat

Figure 35. In the first photograph, Kelly does a somatic variation of the yoga *Little Boat*, turning her knees in one direction and her head in the other. This is an oppo-sitional movement that rotates the spine (especially through the neck) in an evenly distributed way. When she goes back to turning her head in the same direction as her knees, it becomes easier and smoother than before. In traditional yoga, *Little Boat* is held still in the middle. We like to rock the boat, playing with the direction of the head and knees (*Eastwest Workshop,* SUNY Brockport, 2006).

In the second photograph of figure 35, Alycia and Sondra support Meredith in the water in the *Little Boat*. Their hands find the rhythm of Meredith's cran-

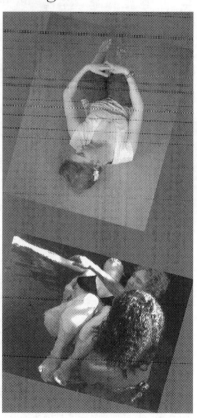

Figure 35. *Little Boat*

iosacral system. This rhythm is slow, flowing, and meditative. Cellular consciousness and embryonic life can be evoked through contacting this rhythm with listening hands. When the little boat tips to the side in the water or on land, it comes to rest in *Embryo*—one of the few side-lying positions in yoga (Photograph by James Holland, *Dancing on your Path Retreat,* Lucky Buck Ranch and Dance Deck, Healdsburg, California, 2007).

Image
Embraced and secure, the little boat floats and rocks in the water.

Benefits
1. Healing the back through movement awareness and giving-in to the floor.

2. Contacting the breath through the legs, as they squeeze in close to the belly on the exhalation, and move away from the belly on the inhalation.

3. Squeezing expansiveness of the pelvic floor.

4. Rehabilitation of the neck in the somatic variation explained below.

5. Evoking cellular consciousness, especially of the floating embryo.

Instructions
1. Hold the knees above the torso; this tilts the pelvis and lifts the tailbone from the floor, allowing the low back to find its full length. This simple position helps space the vertebrae of the lumbar spine and provides a gentle stretch to the entire spine. The floor provides a supportive surface for the movement.

2. Roll incrementally to the side, rocking back and forth, gradually increasing the distance until you come to rest on your side. The back rests in a new configuration on its side.

3. *Somatic Variation:* As a somatic variation, you can take the head in the opposite direction of the roll. This will rotate the

vertebrae of the neck gently if you don't stress the movement. Make it smooth, and roll slowly.

4. After doing oppositional movement, take the head back into the normal turn in the direction of the roll. This will make the roll to the side easier.

Think About

1. Keeping the movement minimal and gradually rolling onto the side.

2. Using your breath to gently expand the boat on the inhalation and to empty on the exhalation.

3. Lengthening the time of the breath slightly, and allowing the low back to rest into the floor.

4. Not pushing forcefully into the breath or the floor, but letting your breath and movement be natural.

Easy Alligator Twist Variation

From The Little Boat, you can rest on your side. There is no single correct way to rest on your side. Try a few versions to find what is comfortable for you. You can also rest easily into the *Alligator Twist* from the *Little Boat* as Sri does below. This is half side lying and half back lying.

Figure 36. *Easy Alligator Twist*

Figure 36. From rocking on her back in *The Little Boat,* Sri simply allows her legs down to one side to float in the *Alligator Twist.* The traditional yoga *Alligator* has various heights for the knees, and also ends with the legs fully outstretched from the knees in this same twisting shape. It also reaches the arms out from the shoulders firmly. Here Sri uses a looser twist, letting her arms rest easily where they feel comfortable. The somatically relaxed moving way of Land to Water Yoga does not insist on replication of a determined shape, but finds shapes through individual adaptation of yoga forms. Somatic yoga respects the individuality of each person, even as it works with the universal givens of the human body (*Land to Water Workshop,* St. George, Utah, 2007).

Back Floating and Pranayama

Figure 37. Back Floating

Figure 37. In the first photograph, Danielle rolls from her side onto her back and floats in back lying, spreading her body into a soft X. She doesn't force her low back into the floor, but lets it express its natural curve. In the second photograph, Sri rests in back lying and pays attention to her breath, lengthening and softening, as she trusts the floor/ ground/earth to hold her. This easy focus on the breath is the basis of meditation (*Eastwest Workshop*, SUNY Brockport, 2006).

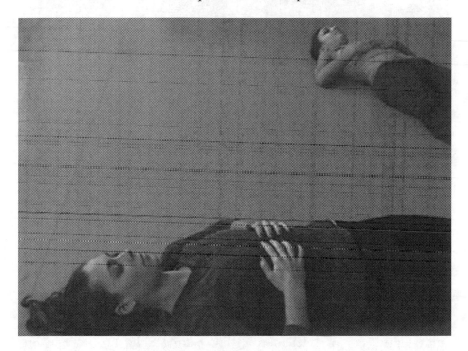

Figure 38. *Pranayama* (*Breath* in Sanskrit)

Figure 38. Jenny (in the foreground) and Erin place their hands on the primary breathing diaphragm as they listen to their breath in back lying. This diaphragm is the third chakra or energy source in the body. Its color is gold. To me, this place of individuation and personal strength represents the power I have to make choices and also to be silent. It is important to know when to take action or speak and when to find comfort and power in silence. The breath is an ocean that supports voice and movement. When it is relaxed and conscious, it is *Pranayama,* the breath of life (*Land to Water Yoga Workshop*, SUNY Brockport, 2006).

71

Figure 39. *Feet in Mountain* (Feet in Standing from Back Lying)

Figure 39. Celine, in the foreground of the first photograph, rests in back lying with her *Feet in Mountain.* She balances her knees over her ankles and keeps her feet more or less parallel. Her heels are in line with her sitting bones. The frame of the body is as wide as the widest point. We see this also in the second photograph, with Danielle. In most people, the frame is the width of the pelvis. The sitting bones are inside the frame, and are false feet, so to speak. They are the feet for sitting. Relaxing with the *Feet in Mountain* allows the entire back to release into the floor, and the low back curve to relax as well. The lumbar spine can elongate in this position and feel itself close to the floor, but it will still express a curve (in most people) unless the pelvis tilts and the tail bone lifts from the floor a little (Celine in the *Eastwest Somatics Hawaii Retreat*, 2006, and Danielle in a *Shin Somatics®* tutorial at SUNY Brockport, 2007).

You can practice a subtle tilt of the pelvis in the *Sea Hose Wave* below.

Pattern 14. Sea Horse Wave

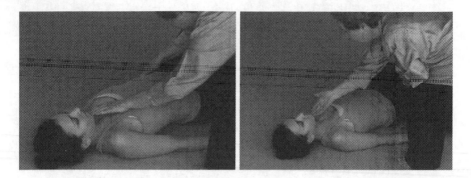

Figure 40. *Sea Horse Wave*

Figure 40. Sondra assists Erin in the *Sea Horse Wave*. Erin has her *Feet in Mountain* as in the previous figure. The chin naturally pulls down during the intake of breath when the low back lifts away from the floor—as in the first photograph. Then the chin returns to neutral (neither lifted nor lowered) on the out breath, when the low back relaxes and comes closer to the floor—as in the second photograph. Sondra's hands help Erin feel the direction of the chin. Sondra is simply outlining the direction of the movement for Erin, not actually moving the chin with pressure (Somatics Class, SUNY Brockport 2006).

Image

In the water, imagine the flowing curves of the sea horse, how the neck curves and draws upward into the head as the chin pulls down. Envision the resonating curves down the back of the sea horse, as it seems all of a piece. Send breath through the flowing golden curves and let them move in subtle waves. Imagine the tail of the spine—the root chakra—initiating the movement.

Benefits

Sensing the spine, neck, and head connected through a subtle wave, as initiated and sustained by the breath and movement of the tail of the spine. Integration, a deep harmony of parts in the whole body, through the wave and the connection of the feet to the floor.

Instructions

1. Bring your feet to stand on the floor with your knees pointing toward the ceiling. This is *Feet in Mountain*. Find balance without letting the knees knock together. Balance can be found when the knees are over the ankles, or the ankles are a little in front of the knees (farther away from the buttocks). The back will come closer to the floor with the feet in standing. The low back may in fact rest into the floor for many people.

2. As you inhale, notice how the low back lifts from the floor, and pay attention to any movement you also feel in the neck. The chin may have a tendency to drop down closer to the clavicular notch on inhalation. Don't force the chin. Just notice how it moves.

3. If the chin lifts up with the *in* breath, instead of drawing down and in, you are probably taking the breath higher up in the back and chest, and not into the low back and belly.

4. This is a very subtle wave, so just let it happen without forcing. The low back lifts away from the floor on the *in* breath, as the chin also draws into the sea horse shape (chin in, head moving up and forward from the back of the neck. You would also hear the direction *up and forward*, for the head, in the Alexander technique).

5. If you can't find the natural wave of this, then see how you can adjust the breath and your movement to find the shape. It will become more natural with time and practice.

6. There is nothing wrong with another breath pattern or wave that you discover with your explorations toward the *Sea Horse Wave*. So if you don't find the pattern I'm describing, just practice what feels good to your neck and spine. The important thing is that you sense the ability of your spine to move along with the breath in an easy wave pattern, without forcing anything. (We give more attention to the movement of the coccyx toward the end of the book in *Chakra Unwinding*, as we consciously add *curling* the hands and the tail of the spine to the image of the *Sea Horse*.)

Think About

Easy movement traveling along the spine with the breath. Pleasure through the body, from the feet in their connection to the floor to the natural rocking of the pelvis as the low back lifts and lowers, resonating up the spine, and neck, and into the head. Think about the total body wave that results from this *Sea Horse* image.

Pattern 15. Rainbow Bridge

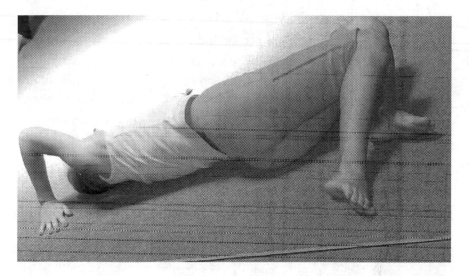

Figure 41. *Side Rolling to Back-Arch*

Figure 41. *Rolling to the side and arching back:* Molly begins to take the crown of her head under the bridge formed by her hand connection to the floor. In this phase of the *Rainbow Bridge,* Molly has not yet moved the back of her head under the arm bridge, so her back is not yet arching into hyperextension. She will achieve this shortly. An arch is a back curve, in this case. Technically speaking, this is hyperextension of the back. Extension would be the full neutral length of the back, not flexed forward or taken back past center into hyperextension. Molly is rolling onto her side and will move into the back arch (hyperextension) as she rolls further.

Image

Arching the entire back with ease. Imagine the arc of a rainbow with bands of color coalescing, dissolving, and then reforming.

Benefits

Bowing (as in a rainbow) the entire body, from the feet in their connection to the floor, through the rolling of the pelvis, to the arc of the
spine, neck, and head.

Instructions

1. Begin in back lying with the knees bent and the soles of the
   feet connected to the ground (*Feet in Mountain*). Sense this as
   a *neutral beginning* to which you can easily return.

2. Connect the right hand to the floor in a *Bridge.* The hand
   goes out to the side of the head with the elbow up. The
   fingers point more or less downward toward the feet, as in a
   full yoga *Bridge* (the asana where the pelvis lifts off the floor
   with weight supported entirely on hands and feet, as the back
   arches high, and the head is upside down with eyes looking
   back behind).

3. Take the neck and back of the head under the bridge of the
   right arm, rolling toward the left side of your body. Keep the
   feet in a rolling connection to the floor, and let the pelvis and
   legs roll to the side as you see Molly doing in Figure 41.

4. Remember, it is the back of the head that goes under the
   bridge, not the nose. So, turn your nose away from the bridge
   (to the left, in this case) and take the crown and back of the
   head under. If you can't get the head through the space of
   the bridge, rearrange your hand connection to the floor to
   provide more space.

5. Let the knees down to the left, as is logical in rolling to the
   left. But don't take them all the way to the floor yet.

6. *Note on flamenco:* In Figure 41, Molly has not yet taken her
   head under the bridge. She is just rolling to the side to free
   her head so the neck can arch back and the head go under
   the bridge. When she finishes the full back arch, she will
   experience something of the ecstasy of a flamenco dancer,
   especially if she pushes through her feet into the floor as she
   rolls to the side.

7. The pelvis has a tendency to push forward as you roll, especially through the connection of the feet with the floor. Enjoy the sensations in your pelvis as it reflects the full arch of your spine.

8. Keep the movement reversible, and return along the same path.

9. Go back and forth under the bridge, returning a few times before trying this on the other side.

10. Keep the movement slow and soft.

11. *Rainbow Bridge:* We are performing a modified yoga bridge with a rolling motion. This bridge is continuously in motion and less stressful than the full yoga bridge. As is often the case in somatic yoga, the emphasis is on moving through shapes rather than holding them still. Let the bridge coalesce and dissolve to its neutral beginning. Alternate back and forth, slowly forming a rainbow bridge and then returning to a neutral beginning, letting the rainbow dissolve into mist on the return.

12. Now put both hands in the bridge and go from side to side. Or save this for another day if you are tired.

13. Finally, take the bridge into a full roll onto the front of the body, and discover a way to return. The latter will require problem solving in movement, or discovery of potentials. Keep this part exploratory, and have fun.

14. Note on a standing version: You can also translate this entire pattern to standing and use a wall behind you for grounding the bridge. Just stand facing away from the wall, and reach one hand back to connect with the wall in the bridge position. Your body will follow through with the rest.

Think About

Keeping the movement easy. Learning as you go and improving without trying.

Frog Dance and Baby Legs Variation

Here is a brief exploration to encourage freedom of the legs, especially the hip joints, and to bring back the joy of your infant-self in learning how to roll over from your back to the front of your body in a playful way.

1. Lift your legs off the floor with knees wide. Balance the legs over the torso.

2. Notice your soft "baby legs" as you remember how babies balance their legs in the air with knees wide.

3. Don't stress the hip joints; just encourage a little freedom there.

4. Begin to roll from side to side, keeping the legs soft and knees lifted high.

5. Find out how you can roll over onto your belly by extending the legs and back.

6. Can you roll onto your front by extending the legs? Notice how they need to somehow accommodate or "get out of the way of the roll."

7. Can you roll onto your belly keeping the knees bent? This is tricky.

8. Roll back and forth from back to front, and then keep rolling in the same direction. Let your body accommodate in any way it needs to for this to happen. There is no right or wrong way, just what you discover intuitively that helps your rolling motions.

Rest either on your front or your back. Pay attention to your breath as it settles.

My Shoulder Loves My Knee Variation

Figure 42. *My Shoulder Loves My Knee*

Figure 42. Meredith in *My Shoulder Loves My Knee*, a *Land to Water Yoga* process, exploring rolling from back lying. (This process can be accomplished from back lying or from sitting.)

From back lying, lift your legs into *The Little Boat*, then cross your ankles. Cross your wrists behind your ankles, and then begin to roll side to side as in the little boat. Let the momentum of the rolling carry you from side to side and keep your head, neck, and shoulders soft. Your head stays relaxed on the floor until it lifts off naturally—as you roll to your side, onto your shoulder, and have the momentum to sit. Your ribs need to fold softly in front, so let your torso relax. See how Meredith's right hand touches the floor here. She can eventually roll onto this hand with more momentum, using the power of the rolling and the planted hand to come up to sitting.

To explore this somatic process from sitting, just begin a play of shoulder to knee, and find out how to get your wrists to cross behind your ankles, and then roll down sequentially—onto your side and then to your back.

79

Eventually, you can roll back and forth from sitting to back lying, but don't try too hard, because trying is self-defeating. Stay present with curiosity, and you will be surprised when your body discovers how to do this without interference from your will (*Shin Somatics® Tutorial*, SUNY Brockport, 2007).

Transition: Jet Lag

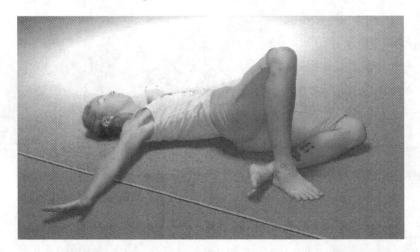

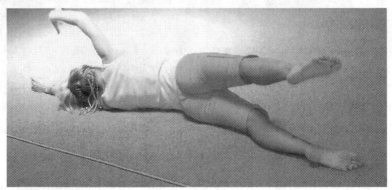

Figure 43. *Jet Lag Transition*

Figure 43. *Jet Lag* is a favorite of students at *Eastwest*. It curves and reaches through the whole body. Because it takes the back into lateral side bending in a C curve, it can be used as a pattern to bring more awareness to the centering of the spine in working somatically with scoliosis. In the first photograph, above, Molly is just beginning to reach for the foot tucked behind. When she connects, this will take her back into a C curve. She lifts her hip off the floor a bit to achieve this. Some people will need to lift more than others. You can lift the hip consciously by pressing the standing foot into the floor with power to stretch through the groin.

1. Begin with feet in mountain, and take the left ankle behind the right leg, as Molly does, above. The next movement is not shown, but is easy to imagine.

2. Connect your right hand to your left foot. This requires you to scoot your back into a C curve, or lateral side bend. Reach down for your foot, as Molly begins to do, above, and let your back curve to the side, so you can take hold of the foot, or at least come near it.

3. Release the foot, and stretch out on your side in a "jet stream," as you see Molly doing in the second photograph.

4. Return by rolling onto your back and bringing your feet to mountain once more. Then do the other side.

Return to Land

Fallen Pigeon

To get a wonderful stretch of the hip area, low back, and pelvic floor: bring both legs up above the chest as in the little boat, then cross the right leg over the left above the left knee. The right leg turns out, with the knee pointing out to the side. This is quite a loose cross, but requires deep flexion in the hip joints. Leave a space between the legs so you can move your right hand into the space; keep the left hand on the outside of the left knee, and grasp it with both hands. Notice once you connect the hands how this position curls the spine, tilts the pelvis, and lifts the tailbone up off the floor. The *Fallen Pigeon* seems difficult at first, but most people manage it over time. Just breathe into the position, remaining where your hands can grasp easily, and let this position do its magic.

If you can't grasp your hands around the top of the knee, go behind it, as you see Molly doing in the photograph below. She is just coming out of the *Fallen Pigeon*, undoing the leg cross, and moving her hands from holding over the top of the knee to behind it. (Holding behind the knee would be *Thread the Needle* in traditional yoga. Molly has just undone the leg cross, so she wouldn't actually be threading the needle at this point.)

You can easily learn the *Fallen Pigeon* position from sitting on a chair: Lift your right leg and cross it over the left at the knee. Now slide the right leg out so the knee is wide, and rest the right ankle above the left knee. The right knee will be wide away from center, and you can look down into the space created between your legs. Reach your right arm into this space. Lean over until you can clasp your hands around the front of the left knee, or go behind the knee if this is a problem.

Fallen Pigeon Recovers

Figure 44. *Fallen Pigeon Recovers*

Figure 44. Molly comes up to sitting through *Fallen Pigeon Recovers.* Holding behind the left knee, Molly will slide her free right leg along the top of the left, moving quickly with friction, and past the left foot, going forward into space until she sits up. It is important that she keeps the connection of her hands around the back of the left knee. The long sliding motion along the top of her left leg will bring her up to sitting, as she continues to hold her hands behind her knee. This kind of "sit-up" teaches you connectivity through your core. It is effortless, fun, and easy after your body understands it as an internal curl. As you come up with momentum, holding behind the knee, your head will lift from the floor, arching momentarily, and then come forward. Your body will curl inward and come up to sitting as a result (*Green Gulch Zen Center Retreat*, Marin, California, 2006).

Easy Side Sit Swivel

A more simple way to come up to sitting is through what I call *The Easy Side Sit* (not shown). From back lying with *Feet in Mountain*, roll over onto your side, and keep rolling until you catch yourself with your hands, and push up to sitting. Let your head be the last part to come up, so you won't strain it forward. If you leave the head to last, you will accomplish a spiraling motion of the spine. With momentum, you can come up through the *Easy Side Sit Swivel* without using your hands. *Easy Side Sit* is a spiraling motion, moving from the back through the side, toward the front and up, whereas *Fallen Pigeon Recovers* moves directly forward into space without turning.

Walking Back

Figure 45. From Crawling to Standing

Figure 45. Above we see how Deborah comes from crawling to standing, as she prepares to come up through a direct path. In the background, we see others coming up through a spiral path.

To summarize the sequence of returning to land, we begin in back lying and move from the last part of the five-part sequence to the first: *Back, Side/Front, Sit, Crawl, Stand.* The simplest way to come up from back lying is through *Easy Side Sit Swivel.* This swivel quickly moves through side lying, and indicates front lying, as it rolls forward and you sit up. After sitting comes crawling, to standing, which can come in many ways.

Running and Dancing

Moving Back:

From the beginning, babies dance. Even in the womb they respond to sound and music. Isadora Duncan and Ohno Kazuo both said they learned how to dance in their mothers' wombs. Parents reinforce the baby's propensity to music, poetry, and dance when they sing to them, cuddle them rhythmically, play gestural touching games like "patty cake," and respond with delight to their little jigs as they learn how to walk.

Figure 46.

Figure 46. The movers break from walking, into running, and then into dance, moving from the energy generated in the feet and legs. Happy infants also dance as they learn how to balance, walk, and run with harmony and rhythm.

Dancing from the Heart Space and Lotus Crown

Through the white lotus crown: This dance moves up from the heart to the crown chakra. Each dancer finds his or her own way of enlivening the upper body, with support from the feet and legs, the foundational root chakra. The arms provide pathways from the heart to the head and to knowledge, as the body sprouts wings (*Hawaii Retreat,* Kalani, 2006).

Figure 47. Sri Dances Freely at the 2008 Hawaii Retreat in Kalani
It's not the head which has wings: it's the heart.[6]

Butoh Improvisations

The following photographs capture something of the *butoh* improvisations at *Eastwest*. They relate to nature and the human energy system and are a dance outgrowth of somatic yoga. *Land, Air, Water, and Fire* live in the body and manifest in dance. Butoh is a metamorphic form of dance that originated in Japan during the last half of the twentieth century and is now practiced globally. Butoh means "ancient dance," and also "darkness dance," as it admits the shadow side of the psyche and morphs toward the light.

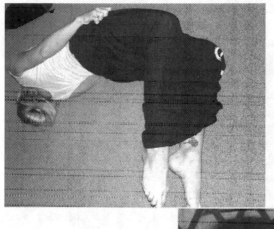

Figure 48. *Butoh Performances,* Molly Snell and Catherine Schaeffer (*Eastwest Retreat: Meditation in Motion,* Green Gulch Zen Center, Marin, California, 2005).

Figure 48. In her *butoh* (the first photograph, above), Molly explores the image of "waiting," until her body arches and rolls from the emotional center, the second chakra in the belly. The color of this chakra is bright orange, and it is liquid in essence. Notice the relationship of Molly's *butoh* to the side-rolling pattern she does in Figure 41. In her *butoh*, she reaches a full arch, balancing in side lying, but without the arm bridge of Figure 41.

In figure 48, Catherine wears a playful collage costume and allows the fingers to guide her in the moment. The fingers (through the hands and arms) extend from the heart chakra. Catherine sits back on her heels and uses gestural movement to guide her. I witness infant curiosity through her dance, the gestural desires of the heart moving through the hands.

Figure 49. Kayoko Arakawa in *Remembering*, Sondra Fraleigh in *Winter Tree for Ohno Kazuo*

Kayoko, in the first photograph of Figure 49, dances from the third eye, the chakra of vision and image, as she remembers her ancestors. Alycia rests into her roots and the tree. James reaches up from the ground, connecting heaven and earth, yang and yin. The body remembers everything, from infancy to the age of breath. Kayoko's dance reminds us that we carry our ancestors in our bones (*Dancing on your Path Retreat,* Healdsburg, California, *Lucky Buck Ranch Dance Deck,* 2007).

In the second photograph of Figure 49, Sondra dances barefoot in the snow from the crown chakra, for her mentor, Ohno Kazuo, on his one-hundredth birthday in 2006. The crown chakra is white and represents the spiritual body. Ohno is the father of *butoh*; he also represents the mother in many of his dances. He danced through the entire history of modern/postmodern dance, new expressionism, and *butoh*. His dance finally transcended all of these genres and designations (Brockport, New York, 2006).

Return to Standing

Figure 50. Return to Standing

Figure 50. Students at *Eastwest* achieve elegant ease in standing, as they practice bringing the head to its horizon. In this photograph they assist each other, using their hands to the side of the jaw and crown of the head, and gently tipping the ribs up in back. Kelly (in the middle) mirrors upright balance as she observes Sondra assisting with her hands. In completing the circle of learning, Sondra finds her own center as she teaches (Somatic Yoga class, SUNY Brockport, 2005.

Chakra Unwinding: Water to Land

The infant's inner sensations form the core of the self. They appear to remain the central crystallization point of the "feeling of self" around which a "sense of identity" will become established.
—Margaret Mahler

I believe that infant developmental stages can be used as a template for moving through the energy system of the body. In yoga, the energetic makeup of the body is conceived as seven life-generating centers moving from the root (feet, legs, and coccyx) to the crown. Anodea Judith defines a chakra as "a center of organization that receives, assimilates, and expresses life force energy."[7] These seven bioenergetic vortexes can be consciously activated through the somatic yoga processes we have been exploring. We have been using a five-stage model, but it is easy to extend this into seven when we think of *Bear Walk* and *Standing Up* as stages in and of themselves. We have been including *Bear Walk* as a transition from crawling to walking, and *Standing Up* we have included as an aspect of walking. We give them their own status here in relating developmental stages to the chakras.

Each chakra develops out of the support of previous ones. Likewise, we see how moving from the back to the front, then up to sitting, kneeling, bear walk, standing, and upright walking is also progressive, ascending through seven energy vortexes. If infant life itself is developmental, in the larger picture of chakra development infancy provides support for childhood, adolescence, and the adult self.

The following movement meditation unfolds a seven-level chakra model of human development through progressive ages from infancy through adult life. It unwinds from the foundation of infant movement and extends toward the adult. While chakras continue to mature and develop throughout life, infancy provides the prototype for everything to follow. *Chakra Unwinding* makes conscious what is taken for granted in infantile unfolding of motor skills. Chakras are not literal entities; rather, they are embodied patterns of psyche, spirit, and universe activated through the physical body. They are first embodied in prenatal life and infancy, but, as indicated in the descriptions below, they develop progressively in life, the completion of one stage supporting the next, as Judith's work makes clear.[8] Typically, the energy system of the body functions as a whole, and not in parts, but we can bring attention to specific parts for the purposes of awareness, integration, and healing.

Chakra Unwinding from Water to Land, as explained below, is also taught and demonstrated in DVD format, available through the Eastwest Institute for Dance and Movement Studies, a resource listed in the appendix.

Seven Stages and Seven Ages

> *One man in his time plays many parts; his acts being seven ages.*
> —William Shakespeare

I like to imagine the body itself as a tree. Its center, the human spine with its rich supply of nerves branching into the whole, gives us the impetus *to grow up*, to grasp and hold with the hands, to give and reach out through the arms. As a dancer, however, my impetus to grow upward is tempered; I remember the ecstasy of the downward spiral. Giving into the earth brings peace and joy, while ascending is heroic and full of awe. See what image arises for you as you unwind the many colors and meanings of the chakras. For me, the process is like the gradual coalescence of a rainbow, with each ephemeral arc of color lifting higher through its connection to the water of prenatal life and the developmental ground of infancy.

In *Chakra Unwinding*, we move toward land from our origins in water, and then up from our roots, as expressed through the feet and legs in relation to the coccyx. Of course, this also involves the floor of the pelvis and the pelvis itself, since the coccyx is part of the pelvic structure— but in the first chakra we focus attention on our vestigial ancient tail. We experience the tail first through floating, then through the pressure of the feet into the ground.

Please move with generosity toward yourself and maintain ease as you move. It is more important to *let* the movement happen than to *make* it happen. Remember that the path to the self is fluid and changing. The movements and positions make use of ascending developmental stages and are simply suggested places to begin. If you have done the processes throughout this book, you have already experienced most of these movements. Become more creative with them as you progress. The color, meaning, and sense of each chakra can be included through visualizations. The sections called "Meaning in Motion" provide guiding imagery for visualizations throughout.

My interpretations of the chakras are informed by the work of Anodea Judith and others, by my meditations at the first ashram of Sri Aurobindo in Baroda, India, and by my research in teaching *Chakra Unwinding* in a variety of situations, including its uses in teaching through touch. The developmental stages of the chakras from prenatal life through infancy and adulthood are articulated well in Judith's work, *Eastern Body: Western Mind,*[9] in which she relates the chakras to psychology. Here I relate them to somatic movement therapy and meditation. In order to get the most from *Chakra Unwinding*, take time to embody it in several sessions. Eventually it will become second nature, and the full sense of it will flower spontaneously. You can also tape record the instructions and visualizations, so you can listen without needing to read them. Teachers of this form are listed in the appendix, and the instructional DVD is also helpful.

1. Unwinding Chakra One from Back Lying

The first chakra relates us to tribe, family, and origins. Like your back, your origin is behind you. It is background as well as ground. As it supports you, your original back is carried into the present and foreshadows the future. What moves forward can also return, easily reversing. Flexibility and reversibility are markers of health in the root chakra. Not getting stuck, the tail moves with freedom, as the rest of the body follows through. We begin in back lying and floating, and then lift the coccyx through grounding the feet. Finally, we arc from the feet to the head through the *Rainbow Bridge.* We take more time at the root to establish wholeness, ease, strength, and flow—unwinding with more speed as we move upward through successive energy centers. The following six-part sequence for unwinding the root chakra can be rehabilitative for the spine, if it is done without stress and kept within a reversible range of motion that is comfortable and pleasurably connected. All of the other chakras depend on the full expression of the root. If the time of your session is limited, and you choose to unwind just one chakra, do this sequence, and let it resonate throughout your being.

Watery Background

1. The *Sea Horse Wave* as explained and illustrated in *Pattern 14* imparts a definitive experience of the coccyx. As you do the *Sea Horse,* attend to the easy grounding and rocking of the coccyx, and note how the pelvis and head rock back and forth easily in relation to the grounding of the feet. Feel how the feet, pelvis, and head are related in the *Sea Horse.* Even as the feet feel the ground, you can bring a floating sensation to the whole image.

2. *Deepening the Sea Horse Wave through Curling:* To vary the *Sea Horse* and bring even more awareness to the coccyx in relation to the entire spine, begin the process by lying on your back with your feet standing; bring your arms down by your sides with the palms up. *Inhale* as you lift the low back from the floor and your chin drops down toward the clavicular

notch; lightly press into the floor with your heels; lift and curl your toes up off the floor as you gently curl your fingers and wrists. *Exhale* when you lift your heels and lightly press into the balls of your feet and toes; uncurl your hands also on the exhalation. Feel how your tailbone lifts off the floor and curls up as your back relaxes into the floor and elongates. The back swims up toward the neck and head, while the fingers extend softly. The open-ended lymphatic system, related to survival and cleansing, flows and seeps more completely with your gentle squeezing, curling, and rocking motions.

Flow: As you repeat the *Sea Horse Wave*, notice that your feet are rocking from the heels to the toes along with the rocking of the pelvis and head, and that the hands and wrists also have a gentle curling-squeezing and uncurling motion. These are not separate motions, however, but naturally flow together throughout the whole. Feel yourself *flow* as a single golden organism in water. Let the wave express your watery essence and bond with embryonic life. As your spinal wave becomes subtler, invite the slow-flowing rhythm of the craniosacral system into your awareness, and let your spine bathe in its sweetness.

Background Colors: Gold and aqua. Picture the golden sea horse, floating upright, surrounded and supported by aqua. Swim softly upward from the movement of your tail to your head.

3. Lift your legs into *The Little Boat (Pattern 13)*. The pelvic floor spreads and opens like a four-petal lotus at the root of the spine in *The Little Boat*. The four petals of the lotus are the two sitting bones at the sides, the coccyx at the back, and the pubis in front. Enjoy the sensation of opening the lotus, as you send breath to the pelvic floor through the stem of the spine. Feel how the breath can move the tailbone, as you continue to float in a watery world.

4. *Easy Alligator Twist:* Lastly, allow your knees down to the side from the *Little Boat*. This will bring you into the astonishing spinal twist that we have already experienced,

the *Easy Alligator Twist*. In the text, you can see this as the variation that follows *The Little Boat, Pattern 13* (illustrated in Figure 36). If you experience any discomfort in the twist, unbend your knees, extending the lower legs until the pressure eases, or just rest on your back with your legs long.

Grounding and Bridging

5. *Lifting the Coccyx into a Bridge:* Now experience your feet firmly pressing into the ground from back lying. With your knees bent and feet connected to the floor, release and lift your tailbone by lifting your pelvis off the floor and clasping your hands underneath you. The pelvis can be in line with the shoulders in a diagonal bridge or lifted into an arch of the spine. Remember to keep your attention on your tailbone––now lifted and pressing upward. Keep your head and neck easy, and don't lift beyond a comfortable line for the challenge in your neck and shoulders.

Root Color: Red. Here you lift the tailbone up strongly into the color red. The root colors move from sunlight and water in the *Golden Sea Horse* to brown in grounding the feet. Then they morph to red as they send energy up through the strength of the legs to the fire of the coccyx and pubis. Red is the color of the root charka, of the coccyx and pubis as they tilt and move in relationship, counterbalancing the front and back of the pelvic floor. Red is also the color of blood. Imagine the life-sustaining warmth and sweetness of the blood surging and pulsing through your body.

6. *Rainbow Bridge*: This pattern takes the bridge through the arms, with pressure from the feet, requiring connectivity and integration throughout the whole of the body. The internal organs and intestines rotate with you, stimulating digestive ease. With the feet still in standing, begin to let the knees easily down to one side and then the other. Go back and forth easily, and notice how the pelvis rolls along with you. Let your head roll also. It can go in the direction it chooses. Finally, roll and arc into the *Rainbow Bridge* as explained in *Pattern 15*.

Colors of the Rainbow: Notice in this rainbow pattern the arching of the back and connection of your feet to the floor, how you feel the strength of your back from head to tail, and pay attention to your spine's ability to extend, arch, and rotate. Feel the ecstasy of *side rolling and back arching*—the magical power of the belly stretching in relation to the back. The front and back of you reach in relation as you roll and arch. This is an expression of strength and survival, of reaching and rolling roundness, being born to all of the colors in I AM.

Meaning in Motion

I AM

Visualizations:

I am a child of the universe with nothing to fear. I deserve to be here. I love my body and take care of myself. I trust my instinctive wisdom.

In the *Sea Horse,* I sense how the base of my spine can curl as my low back lifts and falls. My navel lifts with the *in* breath and drops toward the earth with the *out* breath. Movement radiates from my center, curling and uncurling the tail of my spine. I float upright in watery origins through my entire spine. When my tail curls under, I release upward into my neck and head.

My *Little Boat* rocks gently and smoothly from side to side, as I experience reversibility in movement. What goes to one side can easily reverse and go to the other. My arms embrace my legs, my roots.

Easy Alligator Twists and rolls toward its side, waiting for inspiration with each new breath.

In *Rainbow Bridge,* my body bows from root to crown. *I let go of fear*, as I experience the primal arc of my back. My legs and ancient tail express soft connectivity, resilient strength, and survival. *I let go of fear* when the rainbow disappears, even as I experience the vulnerability of my being.

In resting on my back: My supple feet release all negativity. They say, "yes" to life. My tailbone says, "I can wiggle."

Developmental Stage of Chakra One: Womb to Twelve Months

2. Unwinding Chakra Two from Front Lying

The second chakra enlivens the bowl of the belly and the sacrum (or sacred bone). Sexual expression and physical love develops through the relationship of the first and second chakras. Our sense of relationship to others begins to arise in the second chakra as we mirror likeness and difference. We experience joy and power in the belly.

Dropping into the Navel Root and Pleasure in the Belly

1. *Lazy Lizard Spiral, first side:* The *Lazy Lizard Spiral* is a dynamically relaxed position that allows the belly to drop toward the earth and connect, without the discomfort of being totally flat on the front of the body and craning the neck to the side. The *Lizard* drifts toward one side of the body; it is fully explained in *Pattern 11*. We can connect the unwinding of the first charka to the second very easily through this pattern. From *Rainbow Bridge,* simply roll into the *Lazy Lizard Spiral,* coming to rest on either side of your body. (We will call this "the first side" and repeat it on the other side after passing through the *Sphinx* in the middle). The *Lazy Lizard Spiral* maintains the lush roundness and joyful depth of the body and is actually half side lying and half front. Allow yourself to relax and breathe into your navel root in the *Lazy Lizard.* Let yourself have a belly, as you feel the pleasure of relating your belly's navel to the earth's navel.

2. *Sphinx:* From front lying, lift your chest up off the floor and support your weight on your forearms. The elbows should be right under your shoulders so your arms form a right angle for optimum strength. Continue to send your breath easily into your belly and navel, releasing the weight of your pelvis and belly into the floor. Your legs can rest on their front, easily apart, not taut or stressed. Feel the navel as your center of being and root connection to the earth. This lift of the torso

off the floor in front lying represents the baby's first horizon. Looking out toward others and the otherness of the world, the baby has developed enough upper body and arm strength to lift the chest off the floor while grounding the navel.

3. Lazy Lizard, second side: From the *Sphinx,* let yourself down smoothly into the other side of the *Lazy Lizard Spiral,* and take time to relax into the flow of your spine and downward fall of your belly.

4. Barking Sea Lion: This is *Pattern 10.* Here you can experience the belly as a source of power, rooting the navel to land and water, lowering the head from the sphinx position, and letting the hands fan to the side with power. Feel the barrel-shaped torso, and use your powerful flippers to push, pull, roll, and slap. Bark, and let your voice emerge from your belly.

Color: Exotic orange, morphing from red to gold. The lizard and sea lion bathe in bursts of sun.

Meaning in Motion

I FEEL

Visualization: I feel pleasure. I am at home with my sexuality. I have a creative bond with earth and water. I can relax my belly—roll, stretch, and spiral through my navel. I draw strength from the earth through my navel, releasing the weight of my belly into the ground and inviting the friendliness and safety of gravity. I enjoy the sensual center of my being and release any feelings of guilt as I move my belly. If I were standing up and dancing in a great heavy skirt, I could fling it in wide swoops with the pleasure of my belly.

Developmental Stage of Chakra Two: Six Months to Two Years

3. **Unwinding Chakra Three from Sitting**

In Sitting up, we begin a vertical ascent and free the arms for work and play. Here is where we reach toward our goals, succeed, fail, recover, and experiment. The third chakra develops the will and resides just at the base of the ribs at the solar plexus. It involves intention and the balance between voluntary control and letting go—even as it involves the involuntary responsiveness of the primary breathing diaphragm. I think of this chakra as a great golden dome because of the shape of the diaphragm. I sense how the dome moves just under the heart, gently dropping down on inhalation, stimulating the viscera, and lifting up on exhalation to enliven the lungs and heart.

The diaphragm interdigitates with the psoas muscle—which I think of as the walking muscle, because it connects the upper body to the legs through the spine at the level of the third chakra and the lumbar spine. Thus, in sitting up, we expand the breath in relation to gravity. Indeed, the use of the legs and spine is enlisted in a new relationship to gravity. The arms are free to express themselves in any dimension of space, to reach toward shiny objects of desire, to gather and throw, and to wave.

My Body as the Form of my Will—a Caldron Awake

1. To unwind the third chakra, we come up from front lying to sitting. Ascend from chakra two smoothly, as you sit up into chakra three; experience your head and heart in the vertical dimension, playfully and with pure intent.

2. *Wrist Play:* To work with the suppleness of the arms in relation to all of the abilities of the spine, do *Wrist Play*, illustrated in Figure 21. Through the playful power of your arms and the safety of sitting, experiment with flexing, extending, rotating, side bending, shrinking, and growing up. *Wrist Play* is explained in the text as a transitional pattern between kneeling and front lying.

3. *Dolphin Dive, Dolphin Breach:* Remain in sitting, and extend both legs together to the front. Perform the *Dolphin*, as explained in *Pattern 7*, to concentrate energy in the solar plexus and draw attention to the breath as you flex and extend the spine.

4. *Bending Bamboo:* Sit easily with the legs apart for *Bending Bamboo, Pattern 8*. This pattern uses the arms as they stimulate the power of the diaphragm. Prepare by rubbing

your hands together vigorously to create an electric charge. Take them apart and feel the energy still between them. Wave the arms gently, keeping this energetic connection alive. Let one arm keep track of the other as they wave slowly along the same lines. Extend them high as you Finish. Feel the meaning of "reaching out." Keep the reach soft and alive, like resilient bamboo flowing naturally in the wind. Your entire torso can bend as the arms lead the motion.

Color: Golden Achievement.

Meaning in Motion

I CAN

Visualization: I am able. I lift my arms and let go of shame and any feelings of failure. All my mistakes are swallowed in learning. I can always begin anew. I begin where I am, learn, and build capacity as I move. I can stop anytime and listen to the wisdom of my body. Finding balance between work and play, I don't overdo. My ribs are free to move in any direction, as I play with the abilities of my spine.

Developmental Stage of Charka Three: Eighteen Months to Four Years

4. **Unwinding Chakra Four from Kneeling**

The fourth chakra emanates from heart, the central organ of the body. Kneeling and crawling on all fours requires us to find this center, balancing it through length and depth of the torso on the horizontal plane. In coming up from sitting (in chakra three) to all fours (in chakra four), we carry the spine, heart, and head in crawling. When we crawl, we can experience the pure energy of the heart. As a dancer, I crawl often, bringing awareness to my heart through the power of my arms and through my back, with support from my belly. I practice the connection of the legs into the pelvis and spine, and strengthen the relationship of the arms to the shoulders, ribs, and spine. Expressive, effective crawling engages the whole body in contralateral motions that have carryover in walking and improve connectivity in dance.

The Heartfelt Center

1. *Tiger Crawl* encourages freedom and power in crawling. Practice crawling through the image of the tiger as explained in *Pattern 6.* Let your hands become strong, soft paws and your body become supple. Flow through every joint. Move easily down to sit on your side for a rest, and then return to crawling. Shift weight easily, equally, between your hands and knees. Stay as relaxed as a cat.

2. *Rest in Side Sitting:* Listen to the beating of your heart as it comes into a vertical relationship to gravity.

3. *Dragon at the Well* (not explained previously in the text): From kneeling and sitting back on your heels, lean your entire torso forward and take the weight into your upturned hands and arms. (Don't tuck your toes under, but rest onto the front of the foot.) Lean on the back of your forearms, with the hands and palms facing up and the elbows easily bent. Let your torso and head bow down, with support from your forearms. The dragon's head is hanging into the well, giving up to the waters of life, and letting go any heaviness of heart. *Dragon at the Well* is my adaptation of the traditional yoga *Child's Pose.* It is easier to do and allows more room at the heart space. In *Dragon at the Well,* you can bend down as much as you want to, with control resting on the forearms. The elbows bend, and the back of the arms relax forward into the ground instead of reaching back and resting along the sides as in *Child's Pose.*

Color: Pink wildflowers bloom in a verdant field of green. Butterflies chase the dog's ear.

Meaning in Motion

I LOVE

Visualization: I give my power to the earth, and receive it back. I share my life with others. I am not alone. *Crawling* strengthens my heart and grounds it in purity of being. I find once again how to balance my heart between my knees and my hands on all fours, and how the front and back are related throughout the torso. I learn self-love in crawling, that I need not seek my ground in another. I can experience reciprocity and draw boundaries with love. In *Dragon at the Well*, I let go of grief. When I lift my head and torso to come up on my knees, I open the spaciousness of my heart.

Developmental Stage of Charka Four: Four to Seven Years

5. **Unwinding Chakra Five from Bear Walk**

Bear Walking, the transition between kneeling and walking for the infant, brings attention to the throat and chakra five, allowing it to clear through the downward orientation of the head and the powerful experiment of finding upright balance. In walking on all fours, the head hangs down from the neck, as the throat dips and turns expressively. The bear looks down and then lifts up progressively, using the forces of gravity. The bear's neck is thick, but the human neck is narrow. Create a capacious feeling in your neck as you bear walk.

Clearing the Throat

1. To practice *Bear Walking*, come up smoothly from kneeling by lifting your knees off the floor. Keep your weight on your feet and hands. It is not necessary to straighten the knees as in the related yoga pose of *Downward Facing Dog*. Here, your head is also down, but you move it freely at will and use your creativity: turning around, bending your knees, taking your legs wide apart for balance. Discover strength in your movement. There is not much to it, really, just planting the hands and feet as you go, and letting your head and neck be free. Your hips can be lifted high, or you can sit down toward squatting on your (bear) haunches. Try lifting and lowering your head, squatting a little, and playing with different tempos. See the relationship of *Bear Walking* and *Down Dog* in Figure 13 (squatting is not shown).

2. I like to play with *Bear Running*. I survey the space first to make sure I have room and won't bump into anything. I also like to stagger a little, and sometimes roar. Keep this playful and short, so that it stays experimental and not goal oriented. When things speed up, it is easy to lose track of clearing the

throat chakra. Find a balance between sound, speed, stillness, and movement. Remember to keep the throat free and the jaw easy throughout, like an Olympic runner who practices to keep the mouth and jaw relaxed in the heat of the contest.

3. *Resonance* guides chakra five, as the bear stands up, bristling with potency and rhythm, ready to roar.

Color: The color purple. Red piercing through the blue rays of heaven. Clear amethyst.

Meaning in Motion

I SING

Visualization: I find my voice in many ways, as I represent my world in words, in sound, in movement, and in materials. I communicate with skill and forethought. I listen for the truth and let go of lies. I release feelings of not being good enough. I am complete. I can wear any color. I am an artist.

Developmental Stage of Charka Five: Seven to Twelve Years

6. **Unwinding Chakra Six from Standing**

Standing is a miracle that involves all of the body's balancing abilities, especially the eyes and ears residing at the level of the sixth chakra. At eleven months, the baby negotiates a dance of balance. At twelve months, he combines action and expression through the energetic connections of chakras one through five, extending his use of vision and hearing. In chakra six, he explores boundaries in his environment and balances on two legs. The pull of gravity becomes second nature to him, as he continues to develop an upright stance between earth and heaven. Standing up, looking out at the world, he can relate to others and learn how to walk and dance.

The work of adolescence is also about standing up. The teenager cultivates an independent stance, moving through the awkward and rewarding space of transformation as she separates from parents and moves toward adulthood. Transformation is an apt metaphor for chakra six, as symbolized in the mystical third eye. The adolescent casts herself in the image of her dreams, envisioning her possible self. The issues of standing up return again in the adult, especially in old age where loss of balance is a potential problem. Sometimes adults experience difficulty in walking and need to recover a friendly relationship to gravity all over again. Adults can benefit from somatic processes that aid postural awareness and balance, as described below.

The Miracle of Standing

1. *Mountain:* Stand up from *Bear Walk* to explore the sixth chakra through *The Mountain* asana explained in *Pattern 1.* Begin by finding your full height, and balance on two feet standing in *Mountain.* If standing with your feet close together seems to challenge balance too much, stand close to a prop that you can use, or ask someone to spot you.

2. *Finding Your Horizon:* Add another dimension to the *Mountain* as you find your horizon and bring consciousness to the mystical third eye in between and just above your brows. This is the aspect of the sixth chakra that represents vision, intuition, and immediate knowledge. *Finding Your Horizon* is explained in the text, but, for now, you can practice a short version by standing tall in the *Mountain* and looking out on your horizon, with your chin neither lifted nor lowered. It is important to find an easy balance of the head on the spine, through attention to length in the back of the neck and ease in the throat with the chin being level. From here you can scan the vista all around you, also looking up and lowering your vision to the ground. Return to your horizon to find your full length. Let your head float upward. This is home base in standing, seeing, and hearing—the horizon of your being. Don't get stuck here; remember, this is just a neutral home base out of which any movement can come. Confidence in standing brings awareness of self in relation to others and an abundant world. Practice looking in various directions and coming home to your horizon without getting stuck.

3. *Standing Meditation:* This meditative stance is shown in Figure 12 in the text. Bring awareness to the third eye in the

middle of the head (the pineal gland in the middle of the brain). Let your attention move from your feet upward to the third eye, the crown of the head, and beyond. Trees also stream this wondrous energetic pathway from earth to air. Keep your knees soft in this meditation. This will allow the spine its full and easy length, preserving the natural curve of the low back. Balance the head on the spine as you let it float up. Meditate without expectation. Standing quietly in balance is its own reward.

Color: The blue pearl of bliss.

Meaning in Motion

I SEE

Visualization: I see and am seen; my vision touches the world that touches me. I envision myself as who I am; archetypes speak to me: I am a teacher, a wanderer, an artist, a lover, a seer, and a clown. I can transform myself.

Developmental Stage of Charka Six: Adolescence

7. **Unwinding Chakra Seven from Walking and Dancing**

Chakra Seven is the metaphysical chakra, which develops throughout life, being especially prevalent in the metaphysical questions of childhood, midlife, and old age. Children have a way of reducing the large questions of life to their simple elements. They want to know about God, where babies come from, and what evil is. They are told to be good, so they test the boundaries of being bad. They want to know what happens when we die. Questions of identity arise in midlife, as we review our satisfactions and disappointments. Mysteries abound throughout life, and we learn in spite of ourselves. The world becomes our teacher, and, if we are lucky, it becomes our friend and lover.

In chakra seven, we rest the achiever and give up our longings, attachments, and judgments. Here, at the crown, we find peace and wholeness. We can also practice peace in every stride when we become conscious of our freedom in walking.

We practice the lessons of letting go and prepare for death with equanimity and peace.

Practicing Peace through Non-Attachment and Non-Judgment

1. Simplify the *Mountain Stride* (*Pattern 1,* Figure 4) in this way: Keep the height and horizon of the *Mountain* as you stride forward one small step, and lift the heel of the back foot, keeping the toes connected to the ground. Then, shift to the back foot as you lift the toes of the front foot. You can choose to look down or keep your eyes focused on your horizon. Return to the forward foot and lift the back heel, as in the beginning. Keep the knees soft, and don't bend them. Remember, this is a tall mountain with soft knees and a flexible core.

2. *Walk freely* using the rolling motion of the foot you have just experienced. Feel the lightness of your walk as you let the head float upward from the crown.

3. *Dance,* and allow your walking to morph toward freedom. See how walking becomes dancing so naturally. Improvise your inner dance of the moment; let your feet remember the ground, your legs move in any rhythm, and your arms reach out when it feels right. Tilt, fold, and fall to the ground as you soften your body. Arise at will. Let yourself go into the feeling of the dance, not the look of it. Eros emanates from the first and second chakras as we dance with biological nature—but when we reach the crown, we dance into pure love, not ruled by the senses, but released into ether. From the crown, find your subtle body in relation to the stars and the moon. Empty out and dance. Stop in any position and find the silent meaning of it, without reason, being *in* all of it.

4. *Empty Leg Meditation:* If you want to finish in a quiet mode, try this: Lower your center of gravity by slightly bending both knees, with your feet in parallel. (This is the basic position of the butoh walk, *hokotai*). Keep your torso upright and walk, taking very small steps; as you lift the leg and put it down slowly, empty it out. Leg after leg, practice

slow walking and emptying. Picture this: your leg slightly lifted in front with the foot relaxed and dangling. The support for the lifted leg is your balance on the standing leg. Go even more slowly until you stop with one empty leg lifted in front.

5. Breathe deeply and relax as you take your weight on both legs and find your full height in *Mountain*.

Color: White lotus blossoms drift; droplets form on their flat green leaves floating like large hands on the still pond. A paper boat waits at the edge. Snow falls on the mountaintop.

Meaning in Motion

I KNOW.

Visualization: I will walk till stillness overcomes me, and I am awake.

I attune myself to the cosmos, and allow myself to be moved. I walk in my freedom and wait for wisdom, clearing my mind of its attachments. I dance the perfection of human flourishing and act toward others with kindness and generosity.

Developmental Stage of Charka Seven: Birth to Old Age (Life, Death, Life Cycles)

To Remember

The images that flow in the mind are reflections of the interaction between the organism and the environment, reflections of how the brain's reaction to the environment affects the body, reflections of how the body's adjustments are faring in the unfolding life state … The mind exists for the body, is engaged in telling the story of the body's multifarious events, and uses that story to optimize the life of the organism.[10]
—Antonio Damasio, neurobiologist

"I," you say and are proud of the word, but greater is that in which you have so little faith, your body and its great reason, that does not say "I," but does "I."
—Friedrich Nietzsche, philosopher

What do we gain by understanding the mind in the perspective of the body, and not as an entity that tells the body what to do, as in traditional body/mind dualism? Throughout this text, we have been experiencing the mind of the moving body, remembering our natural bodies in five primary movement stages that elicit surprising infant and childhood memories. And we have been exploring seven stages of chakra development through the related process of Chakra Unwinding. Done with self-awareness, Land to Water Yoga and Chakra Unwinding can heal pain and trauma, bring insight, and instill peace of mind. But the benefits will be lost if goal orientation and stressful habits guide the practice.

As you learn the sequences, practice an easy meditative awareness. Observe yourself without judgment. In this way of learning, there are no mistakes. If it seems you are not getting something right, just let it go, and move on. Return to it later, and see if some new understanding allows you to open to the learning. Renew yourself with each new stage and exploration. Let go of those things that don't seem to work right away. There are many ways into learning; one of them is through observation, just noticing what works best for you and letting the wisdom of your instinctive body frame the potentials for change and growth. Allow yourself to learn through observation and experience, not forcing results.

Likewise, become an observer of your thoughts and emotions. Respect them without getting attached. Work with the changing terrain of your abilities. You will not be the same every day. Let the lessons of this work come to you without great effort. Apply yourself and do your best without stress, understanding that your best will change from time to time. Start with what you understand, and let the learning unwind naturally and with joy. Remember that your body is your best teacher. Listen to your body and its great wisdom.

Appendix I: Glossary and Terms

Frequently used terms in the text that may be unfamiliar to some readers.

Archetype

>A model or life pattern. In psychology, an image or symbol that often appears in dream or myth.

Asana

>A yoga posture or held pose.

Butoh

>A contemporary form of dance that began in Japan in the turbulence of the 1960s and continues to develop internationally. The central aesthetic of butoh is metamorphosis and transformation.

Chakra

>In yoga, the energetic makeup of the body, conceived as seven life-generating centers moving from the root (feet, legs, and coccyx) to the crown of the head. These centers are not literal entities that can be seen. Rather, they are somatic centers of sensation and feeling, sometimes thought of as wheels, or vortexes of energy that receive and generate life. Meanings of developmental aspects are associated with each center as can be understood through the Shin Somatics process of Chakra Unwinding featured in the last section of this book.

Extension

Bringing the spine erect or stretching it long, especially after it has been flexed. Extension is often used for hyperextension, the backward arching of the spine, and it also refers to unbending a joint, or unfolding a joint.

Flexion

Forward bending of the spine, or bending of a joint such as the knee, hip, or wrist.

Image

A picture or likeness of something produced physically in art or conjured in the mind. A representation or embodiment of something in dance, yoga, or movement.

Improvisation

In dance and movement: performing intuitively without set choreography.

Integration

Harmonious relationship of parts. In human movement: balance, coordination, and ease are contributing factors.

Meditation

Any of a number of practices that use sitting or standing still to quiet the mind and to cultivate tranquility and spiritual awakening. Forms also include walking meditations and contemplative dance techniques. Techniques vary vastly from one another and may include chanting, breathing, and counting. Meditation has developed principally in Eastern countries in relation to cultural and religious practices. In the West, it is often pragmatically oriented toward individual growth and personal goals rather than religious ritual.

Movement Pattern

A sequence of movement that can be repeated. Also refers to developmental forms that appear characteristically in nature and in human life.

Phenomenology

The branch of philosophy that studies experience in relation to the body and body/mind theories.

Pranayama

Breath, in Sanskrit, the ancient language of India; sometimes called *the breath of life*.

Psychosomatic

Involving both psychological and somatic dimensions of being. Sometimes used to describe illnesses that are thought to have their origins in the mind or psychological factors such as stress and trauma.

Shin

A Zen word with several related meanings: center/heart/core/ tree trunk/spirit/body.

Soma

The Greek word for the body as perceived by the self. In phenomenology, this would be body-for-self—not the objective body that we observe, but the body we sense subjectively. Thus, body-for-self is the basic somatic reality. *Soma* is also another word for water. If we consider the relationship of these meanings, we can say that soma refers to embodied experience, and to the watery precognitive self. In the nervous system, each neuron is composed of a cell body called a soma, a major fiber called an axon, and a system of branches called dendrites.

Somatic Awareness

Awareness of one's own body, which can be called upon consciously at any time.

Somatic Practices, also Somatics

A field of study and growing body of knowledge based in movement therapy and reeducation, and characterized in several prominent schools and practices. Some are: Authentic Movement Practice, The Feldenkrais Method®, Body-Mind

Centering, The Alexander Technique, and Shin Somatics®. Somatic practices focus primarily on movement for health, awareness, and healing. They include group classes and individual hands-on therapy with the aim of improving function and expression. Somatic hands-on work focuses on movement awareness and repatterning, not manipulation, as in massage. Somatics also refers to a branch of psychology that gives primary attention to depth psychology in relation to perception and embodiment.

Somatic Yoga

Yoga informed by somatic practices. Somatic modalities of yoga acknowledge pleasure and the need to be released from ingrained habits and limiting beliefs in order to heal. Gentle somatic modes of yoga encourage renewal through the relaxation response, self-remembering, and recovery of a more natural, original body.

Symbol

A symbol stands for or represents something else, and often depends on context.

Yoga

Yoga is a Sanskrit (ancient Indian) term for union and integration. It refers to any of a group of related body-mind and spiritual practices developing in the East over thousands of years. There are many systems of yoga, but the general aim is the same: to promote health through stability, energy, flexibility, relaxation, and regeneration. The original purpose of the postures and breathing exercises was to prepare devotees to sit still and remain alert for long periods of meditation. Yoga continues to change and transform in relation to cultural factors. Noncompetitive forms of contemporary yoga promote concentration and psychological resilience, and aim to improve quality of life. The religious practices often associated with yoga have been dropped in many Western forms that concentrate more on physical benefits. This text develops a somatic form of yoga based on developmental patterns, spiritual, and psychological growth.

Appendix II: Teachers and Resources

Shin Somatics® Land to Water Yoga Teachers

Akiko Kishida MA, RSME, RSMT, Tokyo, Japan: somatics@work.odn.ne.jp

Alycia Bright Holland MFA, CMT, Rochester, New York: dancemigration@yahoo.com

Catherine Schaeffer MFA Med, RSME RSMT, Valdosta, Georgia: caschaef@valdosta.edu

Danielle Farrelly BFA, New York, New York: dfar1209@brockport.edu

Dorothy Hanna Feldenkrais®, RSME RSMT, Shreveport, Louisiana: dorothykh@earthlink.net

Elena Shalaev MA, North York, Ontario, Canada: eshalaev@hotmail.com

Jaclyn Moynahan BFA, New York, New York: jaxdance02@yahoo.com

Jeanne M. Schul MA, RSMT, PhD candidate, Rome, Georgia: jeanneschul@bellsouth.net

Jenny Showalter MFA, Brockport, New York: danceshow3@yahoo.com

Karen E Smith, Shin Somatics®, RSMT, London, UK: karen@sense-intelligence.com

Kayoko Arakawa MA, ADTR, Tokyo, Japan: dtkayoko@nifty.com_

Kelly Ferris MFA, Shin Somatics®, RSMT, Hattiesburg, Mississippi: kelly.ferris@q.com

Kim Sifter AA, Shin Somatics®, San Francisco, California: ks_somatics@mac.com

Lani Weissbach MFA, Erie, Pennsylvania: lani_lalita@yahoo.com

Maho Mitani, Shin Somatics®, Fukuyama City, Japan: maho@dt-process.org

Meredith Haggerty MFA, NCMTB, Chicago, Illinois: haggerty@uchicago.edu

Michelle Iklé MFA, Geneva, New York: mikle@hws.edu

Michiko Harada MA, RSME, RSMT, Tokyo, Japan: somatherapy@hotmail.co.jp

Molly Snell MA, College Station, Texas: msnell@hlkn.tamu.edu

Nancy Pigno MA, RSME, RSMT, Rochester, New York: npigno@frontiernet.net

Peggy Suzanne LaCour LCSW-BACS, RSMT, Shreveport, Louisiana: suzanne.delacour@gmail.com

Robert Bingham MFA, Alfred, New York: binghamr@alfred.edu.

Ruth Way, Head of Performance Studies, Plymouth University, Crediton, Devon, UK: r.way@btinternet.com

Sarah Gullo MFA, Rochester, New York: sarahgullo@gmail.com

Sri van der Kroef BFA, Shin Somatics®, RSMT, Santa Barbara, California: svanderkroef@gmail.com

Tamah Nakamura Ph.D., RSME, Fukuoka, Japan: Email: tamah@gol.com

Eastwest Somatics Network

For certified teachers who may have been added since this publication, see the Eastwest Somatics Network Web site: www.eastwestsomatics.net

Eastwest Somatics Institute

For additional somatics resources and workshops, consult the Eastwest Somatics Institute Web site: www.eastwestsomatics.com For questions about Eastwest Somatics Institute, Shin Somatics® workshops, and the certification process, e-mail: workshops@eastwestsomatics.com

Other Titles by Sondra Fraleigh

Books

Hijikata Tatsumi and Ohno Kazuo, Sondra Fraleigh with Tamah Nakamura, Routledge Performance Practitioners Series (London: Routledge Press, 2006).

Dancing Identity: Metaphysics in Motion (Pittsburgh: University of Pittsburgh Press, 2004).

Researching Dance: Evolving Modes of Inquiry, Eds. Sondra Fraleigh and Penelope Hanstein (Pittsburgh: University of Pittsburgh Press, 1999).

Dancing Into Darkness: Butoh, Zen, and Japan (Pittsburgh: University of Pittsburgh Press, 1999).

Dance and the Lived Body (Pittsburgh: University of Pittsburgh Press, 1987).

Book Chapters

"Spacetime and Mud in Butoh," *Performing Nature: Explorations in Ecology and the Arts.* Eds. Gabriella Giannachi and Nigel Stewart (Bern: Peter Lang Publishers, 2005).

"A Vulnerable Glance: Seeing Dance Through Phenomenology," in *The Routledge Dance Studies Reader*, ed. Alexandra Carter (London & New York: Routledge, 1999).

"Witnessing the Frog Pond: Philosophical Inquiry in Dance," in *Researching Dance.*

"Family Resemblance," in *Researching Dance.*

"Agency, Freedom and Self Knowledge in Dance," in *The Perceived Self: Ecological and Interpersonal Sources of Self-Knowledge,* Ed. Ulric Neisser (University of Cambridge Press, 1994).

Articles and Reviews

"Consciousness Matters," *Dance Research Journal* 32/1 (Summer, 2000).

"From Animate Form to Mindful Movement," Essay review of Maxine Sheets Johnstone's *The Primacy of Movement, Dance Research Journal* (Summer, 2002).

"Freedom, Gravity, and Grace," *Somatics: Journal of Body/Mind Arts and Science* (Spring/Summer 1999).

"Chiyoe Matsumoto: Mother of Dance Education in Japan," *Dance Teacher Now* (October 1996).

"The Spiral Dance: Toward a Phenomenology of Somatics," *Somatics: Journal of Body/Mind Arts and Science* (Spring/Summer 1996).

Comparative Book Review: "Volatile Bodies by Elizabeth Grosz and The Roots of Power: Animate Form and Gendered Bodies," by Maxine Sheets Johnstone, *Dance Research Journal* (Fall 1996).

"A Vulnerable Glance: Seeing Dance Through Phenomenology," *Dance Research Journal* 23/1 (Spring 1991).

"A Vulnerable Glance," Reprinted in *Ballet International,* 1991.

"Poetic Body," *Word and Image,* November 1986.

DVDs Featuring the Work of Sondra Horton Fraleigh

Dancing on Your Path
DVD film by James Holland, made in California, and produced in New York. Features workshop dances and Sondra

Fraleigh's demonstration of somatic hands-on techniques. Available through Eastwest Institute. E-mail: Eastwest@q.com

Utah Sunshine
DVD film by Russell Frampton and Ruth Way, made in France and Utah, and produced in the United Kingdom. Features dances by Ruth Way and narration by Sondra Fraleigh from her book, *Dancing Identity: Metaphysics in Motion*. This is a dance film on nuclear testing, based on Fraleigh's stories of growing up in Southern Utah during the 1950s' testing of atomic and nuclear weapons in Nevada— with winds blowing toward Utah. It is dedicated to Heather Horton and all those affected by nuclear testing. Available through Eastwest Institute. E-mail: Eastwest@q.com

Chakra Unwinding
DVD film in progress, available soon through Eastwest Institute.

Land to Water Yoga
DVD film in progress, available soon through Eastwest Institute.

Selected Bibliography

Aranya, H. *Yoga Philosophies of Patanjali.* New York, New York: State University of New York Press, 1983.

Aurobindo, Sri. *Hymns to the Mystic Fire.* Twin Lakes, Wisconsin: Lotus Light Publications, 1996.

Brennan, Barbara Ann. *Hands of Light: A Guide to Healing through the Human Energy Field.* New York, New York: Bantam, 1987.

Bruyere, Rosalyn L. *Wheels of Light: A Study of the Chakras,* Vol 1. Sierra Madre, California: Bon Productions, 1989.

Cohen, Bonnie Bainbridge. *Sensing, Feeling, and Action: The Experiential Anatomy of Body-Mind Centering.* North Hampton, Massachusetts: Contact Editions, 1993.

Damasio, Antonio. *The Feeling of What Happens: Body and Emotion in the Making of Consciousness.* New York, New York: Harcourt Brace and Company, 1999.

———. *Looking for Spinoza: Joy, Sorrow, and the Feeling Brain.* New York, New York: Harcourt Inc., 2003.

Eisler, Riane. *Sacred Pleasure.* San Francisco, California: Harper, 1995.

Farhi, Donna. *Yoga Mind, Body & Spirit: A Return to Wholeness.* New York, New York: Henry Holt and Company, 2000.

Feldenkrais, Moshe. *Awareness Through Movement.* London, England: Penguin Books, 1980.

Fraleigh, Sondra. *Dance and the Lived Body: A Descriptive Aesthetics.* Pittsburgh, Pennsylvania: University of Pittsburgh Press, 1987.

———. *Dancing into Darkness: Butoh, Zen, and Japan.* Pittsburgh, Pennsylvania: University of Pittsburgh Press, 1999.

———. *Dancing Identity: Metaphysics in Motion.* Pittsburgh, Pennsylvania: University of Pittsburgh Press, 2004.

Fraleigh, Sondra and Tamah Nakamura. *Hijikata Tatsumi and Ohno Kazuo.* London, England: Routledge, 2006.

Hartley, Linda. *Wisdom of the Body Moving: An Introduction to Body-Mind Centering.* Berkeley, California: North Atlantic Books, 1995.

Johnson, Don Hanlon. *Bone, Breath, & Gesture: Practices of Embodiment.* Berkeley, California: North Atlantic Books, 1995.

Judith, Anodea. *Eastern Body, Western Mind: Psychology of the Chakra System as a Path to the Self.* Berkeley, California: Celestial Arts, 2004.

Lasater, Judith. *Relax and Renew: Restful Yoga for Stressful Times.* Berkeley, California: Rodmell Press, 1995.

Mahler, Margaret S., Fred Pine, and Anni Bergman. *The Psychological Birth of the Human Infant: Symbiosis and Individuation.* New York, New York: Harper & Row, 1979.

Moore, Thomas. *Care of the Soul: A Guide for Cultivating Depth and Sacredness in Everyday Life.* New York, New York: HarperCollins, 1992.

Nagatomo, Shigenori. *Attunement through the Body.* Albany, New York: State University of New York Press, 1992.

Satprem. *Sri Aurobindo, or the Adventure of Consciousness.* New York, New York: Harper & Row, 1968.

Siegel, Daniel J. *The Mindful Brain: Reflection and Attunement in the Cultivation of Well-Being.* New York, New York: W. W. Norton & Company, 2007.

Silva, Mira and Shyam Mehta. *Yoga: The Iyengar Way.* Foreword by B. K. S. Iyengar. New York, New York: Alfred Knopf, 1992.

Small, Jacquelyn. *Transformers: The Therapists of the Future.* Marina Del Rey, California: DeVorss & Company, 1982.

Stokes, Beverly. *Amazing Babies: Moving in the First Year* VHS. Toronto, Canada: Amazing Babies Videos, 1995.

The Mother. *The Sunlit Path: Passages from Conversations and Writings of The Mother.* Pondicherry, India: Sri Aurobindo Ashram Press, 1984.

Woodman, Marion. *Addiction to Perfection: The Still Unravished Bride.* Toronto, Ontario: Inner City Books, 1982.

Yasuo, Yuasa. *The Body: Toward an Eastern Mind-Body Theory.* Ed. T. P. Kasulis, Trans. Nagatomo Shigenori and T. P. Kasulis. Albany, New York: State University of New York Press, 1987

End Notes

1. The Mother, *The Sunlit Path: Passages from Conversations and Writings of The Mother,* Sri Aurobindo Ashram, Pondicherry, India (Pondicherry: Sri Aurobindo Ashram Press, 1984), 193. The Mother is the female guru and counterpart of Sri Aurobindo, born in Paris as Mirra Alfassa in 1878. She directed Aurobindo's ashram in Pondicherry until her death at the age of ninety-five.

2. *The Sunlit Path,* 193.

3. *Butoh* is a contemporary dance form that grew in Japan through the work of Ohno Kazuo and Hijikata Tatsumi in the latter half of the twentieth century, then became international in its participation. For a fuller account of *butoh,* see Sondra Fraleigh and Tamah Nakamura, *Hijikata Tatsumi and Ohno Kazuo* (London, England: Routledge, 2006).

4. For more on infant movement development, see: Beverly Stokes, *Amazing Babies: Moving in the First Year* VHS (Toronto, Canada, Amazing Babies Videos, 1995).

5. Mira Silva and Shyam Mehta, *Yoga: The Iyengar Way*, Foreword by B. K. S. Iyengar (New York, New York: Alfred Knopf, 1992), 26-29.

6. See endnote number one.

7. Anodea Judith, *Eastern Body, Western Mind: Psychology of the Chakra System as a Path to the Self* (Berkeley, California: Celestial Arts, 2004).

8. Ibid.

9. Ibid.

10. Antonio Damasio, *Looking for Spinoza: Joy, Sorrow, and the Feeling Brain* (New York, New York: Harcourt Inc., 2003), 206.